CUSTOM FORDS

PIERCE RIEMER

&

STEPHEN MILLS

First published 1987

A FOULIS Book

Published by:
Haynes Publishing Group
Sparkford, Yeovil, Somerset BA22 7JJ.
England

Haynes Publications Inc.
861 Lawrence Drive, Newbury Park,
California 91320 USA

Library of congress catalog card number
86-83368

British Library Cataloguing in Publication
Data
Riemer, P.W.
    Custom Fords.
    1. Ford automobile   2. Automobiles –
    Customizing
    I. Title   II. Mills, S.J.
    629.2'222   TL215.F7

    ISBN 0-85429-581-X

Editor: Robert Iles
Page layout: Chris Hull
Printed in England by:
J.H. Haynes & Co. Ltd.

Contents

CUSTOM Fords

Introduction

The intention behind the writing of this book was to examine some of the reasons for the continuing popularity of customised and hot-rodded Fords. Little did we realise how many and varied were to be the influences that have helped shape the styles and trends of innumerable modified Fords over five decades.

It wasn't until Henry Ford made motor cars affordable that anyone even contemplated "individualising" one. Cars were for the rich and powerful. If they wanted an individually styled car, it was ordered from the coach-builders, not constructed with their own hands. When the Model T began to become available to the masses, it was only a matter of time before people began to tinker with them. Initially this was for purely practical purposes. Perhaps it was to carry more people and luggage or perhaps it was modified to suit some particular terrain or set of conditions. As time went by, people began to modify Fords in different ways. Initially they stripped them down and hotted-up the engines in order to race each other on the streets, dirt-tracks and later, lake beds and drag strips.

Others began to modify their Fords with an eye to looks, rather than all-out performance. Starting in small ways, this trend eventually culminated in incredible body modifications, in some cases, making the car unrecognisable as a Ford. If this was the case, the "customiser" had succeeded in creating his own car, even though under the skin it was still a Ford. Sometimes the styles and ideas of these two factions, the go-faster and style-related groups, overlapped and complemented each other, other times they were diametrically opposed. Sometimes they were great friends, other times they were scathingly sarcastic about each other. Throughout all of this there was still the common denominator of Ford cars, in both cases their modified pride and joy, but in totally different ways.

Styling ideas of these two early groups were to develop and expand with the passing of the years. The hot-rodders stuck to their older cars and continued to make them go faster while the customisers carried on cosmetically modifying the newer cars as they emerged.

While this was happening in America, Britain remained largely untouched by it all. Although Britain has had a long history of individually built "specials", there was nothing of the scale of the action taking place across the Atlantic. It was not until the passing of the post-war austerity period that there was the first glimmering in Britain. The occasional hot-rod began to appear, often crude in comparison with its American cousins. They had already been developing their ideas over several decades.

Customs were to appear later still, although for many years, the British idea of the ultimate custom was a Mk I or II Zodiac with every conceivable accessory tacked on! Once again, there was little love lost between the hot-rodding and custom camps.

It was the appearance in the early 1960s of the first few American dragsters to be seen in Britain that would ultimately close the gap between the two, as it also seems to have done in America. Not only did old cars get modified to race at the drag strip, but also newer ones. There were certain modifications that became common to both types of car, with the result that there gradually developed an overlapping of styles and techniques. Not surprisingly, the styles of the drag strip were soon being emulated by innumerable street driven cars, thus making the divide between the rodders and the customisers much narrower.

Recent years have seen the gap largely disappear as, in the face of attempts to bring in hostile and restrictive legislation (in both America and Britain) with respect to modified vehicles of all types, there has been a joining of the ranks against these moves.

Today, rodded and customised Fords are as popular as ever. One of the foremost British magazines recently published its top feature cars for the year and of all the cars included, 60% were Fords. In America, the car magazine with the world's biggest circulation recently picked its top ten cars (out of thousands). Of those chosen, 90% were Fords! Clearly, Ford products still predominate. There does not appear to be a single Ford model that has not been customised or rodded in some way. Every model has its devotees.

It seemed appropriate to examine some of the roots of these peculiar forms of automotive expression, as the history of Ford itself is so inextricably intertwined with them. Why did we decide to include a brief history of the Ford Motor Company? To the uninitiated, it may come as something of a surprise to find that some of those with the greatest interest and knowledge of their particular car and its history, are often the rodders and customisers. Despite the fact that both will happily alter much of Ford's original specifications, each still has a great respect for its lineage. The history is deliberately selective and attempts to reflect the particular periods and models that have played the more prominent roles in the development of these trends. In the following chapters, we have attempted to examine the main influences that have helped to shape today's large and active rodding and customising scene in both

CUSTOM Fords

America and Britain. We deliberately did not include many American cars as these have been well covered in a number of other publications, preferring to examine the indigenous versions to be found in Britain. The majority of examples shown, are regularly used on the roads and thus we felt that these represented the most appropriate selection. We have purposely avoided too many staged, studio shots, preferring to film the cars in their "natural habitats". For convenience, we have split these into appropriate eras. We have included examples from the early part of the century up to, and including, the current trend of body styling kits.

Over a lengthy period, we have examined the British scene and discovered that it now consists of a wide assortment of models, from over a wide span of years and modified in a multitude of different ways. At both British and American events, rods and customs now mix in a way that would have been unheard of a decade ago. Whatever the reason behind this softening of attitudes, it is a good omen for the future. Future years will probably see the rod and custom camps facing many more problems in a world that seems determined to enforce uniformity on many aspects of life, not the least of which is on the roads and highways. They have faced many such challenges in the past, and in most cases, have survived them.

Let us hope that this fascinating and colourful form of automotive art is never destroyed. At the moment, the future looks fairly bright, but who knows what tomorrow will bring. Hopefully it will bring more rods and customs, the majority of them still being based on Fords.

CUSTOM Fords

This book is dedicated to our wives

Christine and Elizabeth

CHAPTER ONE

A brief history of Ford

Early days

Perhaps one of the single most important events in Henry Ford's life occurred when, on a visit to Detroit, he saw Dr. Otto's stationary engine on display. Clearly the event had a profound effect on him for shortly afterwards, at the age of 27, he left the family farm, moved to Detroit and took a job with the Edison Illuminating Company. There followed a period of development and experimentation, ultimately culminating in the production of his first car. Following the limited success of this, he refined his ideas and techniques and built a second. Before long, the "Detroit Automobile Company" was launched to produce and market it. The company had been founded by Henry Ford and a number of like-minded associates and it wasn't long before he had given up his job with Edison, who were none too keen on his passion for automobiles, to become a full-time car builder.

For various reasons the fledgling company foundered and Henry Ford took the remarkable decision, at the tender age of 38, to leave the company and take up a career as a racing car builder and driver!

His first racer was built with the aid of his mechanic, Ed Huff, and was, to say the least, very crude. It was powered by a flat twin-cylinder engine that displaced a total of 540 cubic inches, or nearly nine litres! The monster produced a mere 26 horsepower but in a much-publicised race in October 1901, it still managed to beat the only other competitor, the Winton Bullet. This was to be Henry Ford's first and last victory as a racing driver.

His next venture was in collaboration with Tom Cooper, a former motorcycle racer. Two cars came out of their partnership, a pair of Ford-Cooper specials named "999" and "Arrow". Both cars were of around 18 litres capacity and were raced on a number of record-breaking occasions. In 1903, "Arrow" was used to break the standing land-speed record, the course being run across the surface of a frozen lake bed. Despite the obvious disadvantages, Ford managed to raise the record to a very creditable 91 mph. The legendary American racing driver, Barney Oldfield, was later called in to handle the driving chores.

This period in Ford's early history, although perhaps unusual by today's standards, none the less served to keep the Ford name in the headlines and helped to establish him as a force to be reckoned with. His conviction was that the public expected him to win races and on the strength of that, would go out and buy his cars. He was subsequently proved to be quite correct.

The year 1903, in retrospect, was to be one of profound significance. In this year Henry Ford founded the "Ford Motor Company" following a number of earlier unsuccessful attempts to do so. The company was formed on June 15th with cash assets of $28,000. Having tackled the problems of breaking records and winning races, he now set about the problems of automobile production with typical thoroughness. As early as 1904 he began to look farther afield than the domestic market and in that year began to export to Britain, albeit in a small way. The subsequent formation of the Ford Motor Company

A pair of Ford's finest. Two long-term survivors of the car on which the Ford Motor Company's fortunes were based, the Model T. In total, nineteen million Ts were built between 1911 and 1928, a remarkable production run of nineteen years. Around 275,000 were built at Trafford Park in Manchester. These two beauties were spotted at a Ford rally, still going strong in 1986.

(England) Ltd. was something of a combined effort with Ford of America holding 60% of the company and Percival Perry with his associates, the other 40%. Perry held the franchise to market Ford products throughout Europe.

The Model T and its successor, the Model A. The latter was a much more stylish and substantial car and, in keeping with American practice, was available in a variety of body styles. Following the end of T production at Manchester, the Model A and its smaller engined brother, the AF, were assembled there. The right-hand drive British versions were powered by either a 24 hp four-cylinder side-valve or small-bore version rated at 14.9 hp. A total of 4.8 million As were built, 15,000 of them coming from Manchester between 1928 and 1931.

This period saw the emergence of a number of cars: The Model F, Model S, Model N and the Model K, the latter selling for the princely sum of $2500. Clearly, at the time, the automobile was still very much the plaything of the wealthy, a situation that Ford was neither happy with nor willing to tolerate. His vision of the "affordable automobile" was now close to becoming a reality. In this year the total output of all of the American car manufacturers combined did not amount to much over 32,000.

If 1903 was an important year, then 1908 was even more so, for this year saw the production start-up of the car that was to establish Henry Ford as one of the single most influential figures in the history of the motor car. The car that was to change the way of life of millions of people had been born. The Model T had arrived!

The first year's production came to 8000 vehicles, a very sizeable chunk of the American market to be wrested so quickly from the hands of his competitors. If only they had realised that this was but the thin end of a very large wedge! Before 1909 was over, production was up to nearly 2000 cars a month.

In 1910-1911, Ford began to put himself on a firm footing in Britain with the foundation of the first overseas factory at Trafford Park, Manchester. British car manufacturing was in the hands of a multitude of small to medium sized concerns and within a few years, Trafford Park had been built up sufficiently to become Britain's largest motor manufacturer. The annual output eventually amounted to around 3000 Model T's. 1911 saw Henry Alexander May drive one of Trafford Park's Model Ts up Ben Nevis, a feat he was to repeat in 1928 with a Model A!

Meanwhile, back in America, Ford had

begun experiments with the "moving-line" principle of assembly. Initial trials centred around the assembly of the magneto for the Model T and so startlingly successful were the results that full assembly line production was introduced early in 1912. This was to set the trend that all other motor manufacturers would eventually follow. From the first year's 8000 Model T's, production climbed to nearly 200,000 in 1913.

The assembly line techniques meant that a Model T could be assembled in a matter of minutes, but even at this pace, there was no way that the public demand could be met. Ford's often quoted and misquoted remark of "any colour as long as it's black" stems from this period, as in an effort to speed up the painting stage, black became the only colour offered simply because it dried faster than the alternatives!

Production rates gradually increased as lines were speeded up and assembly line techniques streamlined and simplified. By the end of 1914, over 300,000 Model Ts had rolled through the doors of the Highland Park factory. Model T production was by no means limited to America as many thousands were shipped out in "knock-down" form for assembly at various overseas plants. A large number were produced for the war that was, by now, raging in Europe. Despite the war, production rates steadily climbed and in 1915 the millionth T was built. 1916 saw the production of nearly 590,000 and 1917, more than 834,000.

With the passing of time it became apparent that the Highland Park factory was incapable of sufficient expansion to cope with demand and in 1919 Ford purchased a large new site on the River Rouge near Dearborn. In the same year he bought out the other stockholders in the Ford Motor Company for 100 million dollars!

Ford's major overseas assembly plant was still at Trafford Park although production rates were very small compared to those back in America. In 1911, the Manchester plant built 1500 vehicles and in 1912, just over 3000. To put things in perspective, the output from the Highland Park factory in 1912 alone was

over 82,000.

It has been estimated that by 1920, around half the motor vehicles in the world were Model Ts. The ratio in Britain was only slightly lower with the Model T taking around 40% of the market. This situation, at least in Britain, was about to alter dramatically as, in 1920, the government completely changed the basis of motor vehicle taxation. The newly introduced

An example of a Model A Sports Saloon, one of the many body styles available. Although similar in looks to the Cabriolet, differences include a visor and fixed hood. This car has a few incorrect pieces, such as headlights, however it is still an excellent and uncommon restoration. Mechanically there were few differences between models.

A well restored Model A van. The commercial vehicles of the time often shared similar sheet metal to the passenger car line. Later British-built commercials often featured a variety of parts and panels from earlier car production, presumably until supplies ran out. This applied to both vans and trucks. The American market had a much wider range of commercials, the British options being far fewer. This particular van was brought back to life by its present owner.

A fine example of a model C Deluxe with uncommon touring bodywork. The Model C was produced alongside the Popular and was powered by an 1172 cc side-valve four. The C was more luxuriously appointed than the rather spartan Y and also benefited from extra passenger room. Apart from the tourer, a two or four-door saloon was also available. This car is a regular of the rally scene, shown here at a vintage gathering in Gloucestershire.

CUSTOM Fords

"Motor Car Act" taxed cars at £1 per RAC horsepower, replacing the original system which had been based on a Carriage Tax linked to a high petrol tax.

The effect on the sales of the 22 horsepower Model T was dramatic with sales tumbling almost overnight. For many years, Henry Ford remained convinced that the Act was aimed directly at his beloved T and he may well have been correct in his supposition.

Within a year, the development of long-stroke engines had surged ahead, setting the pattern of British engine manufacture for many years to come. Ironically, it was not until after the introduction of the Act that the T became available in right-hand drive form, all those previously supplied to the British market being of the left-hand variety. Despite the setbacks on the British market, in 1923 Ford arranged the purchase of a Thames-side site at Dagenham with the ultimate intention of a much more sizeable base from which to serve both the British and European markets.

In America, production rates still soared. In 1922 alone, over one million Ts were produced and in the same year, the highly prestigious, but ailing, Lincoln company became part of the growing Ford empire. Following the introduction of their new 5.8 litre V8 engine, Lincoln had fallen on hard times and been forced to turn to Henry Ford for help. After some consideration, he bought out the company for eight million dollars and before long, his son, Edsel, had been installed at the helm.

Meanwhile, production of the T peaked at around two million in 1923, however, the end was coming into view, the last big year for sales being 1926. Ford's main rivals, Plymouth and Chevrolet, were making numerous advances both mechanically and cosmetically, the result being an erosion of the T's market. Although Henry Ford was reluctant to admit it, the Model T was reaching the end of its life and on May 27th 1927, production ceased after an astonishing nineteen year run and more than fifteen million vehicles!

The arrival of the Model A

Following the end of T production there was an agonising six months wait before its successor was introduced in the shape of the Model A. During this time the main assembly line was moved to the new Rouge River site, the first Model A being ready in late October.

The A was a much more stylish car, the design of which had been modelled on that of the elegant Lincolns. Edsel is largely credited with the design of the A, which compared with the T, looked a much more durable and substantial car. By the end of 1928, over 800,000 As had been produced, many going for export, and by early 1929 the millionth vehicle had been reached. Production rates at the new Rouge River plant during 1927 had peaked at nearly a thousand a day, the output having virtually trebled in less than twelve months.

The years 1929 and 1930 were good ones for Ford of America as they dominated the market, outselling their main rivals. In 1929, sales exceeded 1.3 million Model As while the figures for 1930 were still well over the million mark. A number of cosmetic and mechanical refinements were made during 1930, but the then near-obsolete four-cylinder engine was still retained. This era saw a number of publicity stunts, one involving a Model A Roadster being driven backwards from New York to Los Angeles, a distance of 3340 miles!

In Britain, the Model A was in a bad position from the start, the effect of the motor taxation system being exactly as it has been for the T. Ford's answer was the introduction of an under-bored engine, known as the AF, that was rated at 14.9 horsepower. The resultant car was rather underpowered for its size whereas the 22 horsepower car was very expensive to tax. It was a "no win" situation. Clearly the taxation system favoured long-stroke, narrow bore engines, the majority of which were of British manufacture.

Although the building of the huge Dagenham site had started in 1929, because of numerous construction problems, the Model A had much closer links with Manchester. In the early days of the Dagenham plant, however, the main production centred around the Model AA truck. A reorganisation of marketing resulted in England becoming the major European centre with thousands of As and AAs being sent out, both completed and in knock-down form, for reassembly at various European plants. Overall the Model A could not be considered as an outstanding success in Britain.

Despite the A's proven reliability and ruggedness, the American public, in particular, were becoming increasingly aware of improvements in engine design, such as with Chevrolet's AC six-cylinder. Both Chevrolet and Plymouth were beginning to leave Ford behind in terms of style, refinement and engineering.

As the decade ended, sales of the Model A began to drop dramatically. Chevrolet and Plymouth began to take large chunks of the market as the public were swayed by the long list of advantages over Ford. Smoother and more powerful engines, hydraulic brakes, better suspension, the list seemed endless. The plain truth of the matter was that in terms of engineering and technology, the A was lagging far behind. To make matters worse, it was also getting to look a little old-fashioned.

In the face of such competition Ford moved surprisingly slowly. By 1931, as sales of the A continued to plummet, it became quite apparent that a new car was desperately needed for 1932. Clearly, Ford was going to have to move fast or risk the same fate as many of his smaller rivals who, as a consequence of the Depression now gripping America, had gone to the wall. When production of the A was called to a halt after a four year run, it had achieved sales of 4.8 million, in nine different body styles.

The picture was not as black as it may have seemed for, shrewdly, Ford had already set a small team of engineers to work in great secrecy, on the development of what came to be seen as one of his greatest triumphs.

The Affordable V8

1932 was one of those milestone years in Ford's history for in April, Henry Ford unveiled what was both his best kept secret and one of his greatest technological achievements, the "affordable V8" that was to serve him well for the next twenty years. Working against great odds, his engineers had managed to simplify the construction of the V8 by combining the block and crankcase in one unit. All other V8's of the time were assembled from a number of separate castings, the result being a much more complex, hence expensive, engine. This clearly limited them to the more luxurious, expensive end of the market. Ford's engineers had successfully managed to develop the single casting concept thus reducing manufacturing costs enormously. Even when the V8 had gone into production there were still numerous problems to be overcome, such as poor casting reproducibility and overheating. One by one, these problems were solved as the engineers came to grips with what was still unknown technology.

The final configuration was a 90° V8 side-valve, displacing 221 cubic inches, with a cast iron block assembly. The stroke was 3.75" and the bore 3.062". At 3400 rpm, it produced around 65 bhp, a very respectable figure and unheard of in such a low-priced car. The V8 was to remain essentially unaltered for the next twenty three years.

The new V8 was first offered in the new Model 18 which was identical in appearance to its four-cylinder counterpart, the Model B. Such was the public enthusiasm for the V8 that it rapidly outsold the four-cylinder car in the ratio of 3:1. Before long the four-cylinder option was dropped in America.

Despite the public demand, Ford was not yet out of trouble as continuing production problems led to a severe shortage of V8s, this being the main reason for their huge

CUSTOM Fords

losses in 1932. The period was also an important one for Britain, as October 1931 saw the transfer of total production from Trafford Park to the new Dagenham site in a single weekend. The entire transfer took place over a 48 hour period so that no production was lost. Dagenham was now the largest and most advanced vehicle manufacturing complex outside America. The Model B was soon in production and was offered in Britain with two four-cylinder options. There was a 24 horsepower engine as well as an under-bored 14.9 unit, as with the Model A. Clearly the larger engine was more expensive to tax.

The first Model B rolled out of Dagenham at the beginning of May. Because of the disadvantages of the taxation system however, no Model 18s (with the V8) were ever to be built there. The Model 18s which did appear in Britain arrived as rolling chassis from Ford's Canadian plant at Walkersville.

Dagenham, as well as housing the Ford motor company, was also home for Briggs Motor Bodies and the Kelsey-Hayes Wheel Company who produced wheels and hub centres for Ford. Briggs supplied and painted bodies for the plant including those for the rolling chassis imported from Canada. In America, they also supplied Plymouth as well as Ford. Briggs bodies were of a wooden frame-work, clad with welded steel panels and were renowned for their strength. Many bodies (in untrimmed and unpainted form) were also shipped overseas to other assembly plants.

The American plants produced the Model 18 and B in fourteen different body styles. Credit for the design was generally given to Edsel Ford and Eugene Gregory, however, some of the body designs were by the coach-building firm of LeBaron,

Briggs undoubtedly being involved with some of the others. In Britain, almost all models were of the Tudor and Fordor variety, with a few others imported in small numbers.

The first British Ford

As with the Model A, the sales position of the Model B and its variants, was not good and when production finally ceased in 1935, less than 10,000 had emerged from Dagenham. A mere 900 of these were Model 18s. The dire position that Ford of England found themselves in made it clear that fitting American-styled cars with small engines was not the appropriate formula for the British market. Most of the other popular cars in Britain were much smaller and it was with this in mind that Percival Perry asked the main plant for a small economy car, suitable for the more modest requirements of the British market.

The new car was designed by Eugene Gregory and a prototype car quickly built and put on display at the Albert Hall in February 1932. In August, the Model Y, as it was to be known, went into production at Dagenham, the first all-British Ford car.

The little Model Y was an immediate success and over the next year pulled the company back from the brink of disaster. The first Y looked somewhat similar to a scaled-down Model B and was powered by a 933 cc side-valve engine. It produced 22 bhp at 3700 rpm and had a 3-speed gearbox. Suspension was by means of the usual transverse springs. Although unchanged mechanically, the Y was slightly re-styled during the summer of 1932 and again in 1933. The screen was raked back, the bumpers and grill altered and a four-door version made available. The Y proved to be immensely popular and by 1934 had captured 54% of the under 9 horsepower market. From 1935, the Model

A 1939 American Model 91A Deluxe. The power was provided by the long-running V8, this version producing 85 bhp. Following Edsel's long fight with his father, it became the first Ford to be equipped with hydraulic brakes. In keeping with American practice, the grille area and frontal sheet metal of the Deluxe differed from that of the standard model, a trend that was kept up for many years. Not surprisingly, few of these cars found their way to Britain.

Below: **Both Model Ys, but with a difference. The farthest car is a 1932 model, the nearer, a 1933. The car was restyled for that year becoming the "long radiator" model and apart from the difference in grille, other distinguishing marks include the skirted wings and dipped bumper. The earlier Ys resembled a scaled-down Model B whereas the later ones bore more than a passing resemblance to the American Model 40. Although they differ cosmetically, there were few mechanical differences between them. The Model Y was the first all-British Ford to be produced at the new Dagenham complex and saved the company from financial disaster.**

A Ford Model 62, produced at Dagenham. The car was first introduced in 1936 and was powered by a small-bore version of the V8, displacing 2227 cc and rated at 22.1 hp. The Model 62 was a replacement for the American-styled Model 60 and was completely British-built. Unlike the American market, the only option was a saloon version although chassis were available for specialist coach-builders. Only minor alterations were made to the car during its production run.

Y became known as the "Popular" and in the face of competition from other British manufacturers, economy measures were taken and the price reduced to a mere £100. The "£100 Ford" was the first fully equipped, four seater saloon, to be offered at such a low price and remained in production up to 1937 after which it was replaced by the Ford 8.

For much of its production run, the Y was available as a two or four-door saloon and a 5 cwt van, although rolling chassis were available, resulting in a number of special coach-built versions. In Britain, a total of 136,000 cars and vans were sold. Its popularity eventually spread far beyond the coast of Britain and various forms were built as far apart as Germany and Japan.

The advent of the little Y and its great success showed clearly how the British and American markets had diverged and would rarely meet again. One notable and unexpected spin-off was the spawning of its larger American cousin that came, over the years, to be held as the best looking Ford of the decade, the Model 40.

The story goes that Edsel, having seen Gregorie's designs for the Model Y, was so impressed with its sleek, racy looks that he immediately ordered the design of a full-sized version for the American market. This emerged in 1933 as the replacement for the Model B/18. The following year saw a number of refinements and restyling touches, the 1934 Model eventually becoming one of the most sought after 30s Fords.

The Rouge River plant produced the Model 40 throughout 1933 and, with a number of fairly minor alterations, well into 1934. The V8 engine was largely unaltered, the four-cylinder option having been dropped in 1933 as a result of abysmal sales. The British market did not have an equivalent to the Model 40, production of the Model B carrying on until 1935.

Pre-war times

1935 was a good year for Ford with great commercial success around the world and especially on the American market. From now, up to the advent of the Second World War, a host of new models were introduced, many however, being merely face-lifted versions of the previous year. This period saw the introduction of several cars from Dagenham which were, as with the Model Y, specifically designed for the European market.

In America, the new Model 48 appeared, powered by a 30 horsepower V8. As with most of the full sized Fords of the time, it did not sell well in Britain because of the motor taxation system. The Model 48 boasted a new body and a substantially new chassis but fundamentally it was very similar to its predecessors and still retained transverse springing. The Lincoln division of Ford was by no means idle, for this year saw the introduction of both the Customised Continental and the cheaper Mercury.

Britain got an identical looking equivalent to the Model 48, known as the Model 60. This had a lower taxation rating as it was powered by a small-bore V8 of 2227 cc, producing 22 horsepower.

The more modest needs of the British market were, once again, met by the introduction of a car that looked suspiciously like a scaled-down version of the 1935 American Ford, the 10 horsepower Deluxe Model C. The car was powered by a bored-out version of the 933 cc engine, now displacing 1172 cc and producing 32.5 bhp. The C was roomier and more luxuriously appointed than its stable mate, the Model Y, and proved to be a very popular car.

The following year saw the arrival of the American Model 68, available in no less than 16 body styles, all powered by the 30 horsepower V8. The British Model 60 received new Dagenham-produced bodywork to become the 62, this now continuing virtually unchanged up to the outbreak of World War II. Over this period, sales in Britain amounted to around 12,000, the 62 only being available as a saloon or chassis unit. The Model C continued in production and became available as both a two and four-door saloon and a tourer. The grille was restyled to have three vertical openings and the bonnet sides vertically louvred.

1937 saw the debut of American Models 78 and 74, identical except for engine capacity. This year's restyling included a new V-shaped grille, that resembled the Lincoln Zephyr of 1936, with the free-standing headlights now flared into the wings. The location of the water pumps was changed and at last the cooling problems

Below: **An example of the Ford 10, the successor to the Model C Deluxe. Introduced in 1937, it was a typical example of what Ford were producing for the British market at the time, featuring their usual mechanical layout, torque-tube transmission and transverse springs. The power came from an 1172 cc side-valve coupled to a three-speed gearbox. Available in both saloon and tourer form, the car had a new three-slot grill as opposed to the single opening of the 8.**

Above: **A fine pair of Ford side-valves. These gleaming examples of the Prefect and the later 103E Popular were caught at a vintage show in 1985. Although differing in their body style, mechanically they are similar, both having the usual side-valve engine, torque-tube and transverse springs. The Prefect, in its various forms, was a four-door model whereas the Popular was only available as a two-door.**

that had beset the V8 since its introduction, were overcome. Not surprisingly, only around 4000 were sold in Britain, a legacy of the motor taxation system once again. This was the first year that the fabric insert tops disappeared on the American models giving way to solid tops.

Dagenham was not idle and this year saw the Model C restyled to emerge as the Ford 10. Mechanically there were few changes from its predecessor. The Model Y Popular also came to an end in 1937, being replaced by the mechanically similar Ford 8. It still retained the traditional transverse springing and was powered by the 933 cc side-valve engine. Both the 8 and the 10 were specifically designed for the British market and were to be the forerunners of a series of cars that, under the skin, were very similar and destined to span the next two decades.

17

Right:
A further example of a well restored Pilot. A number of these stately cars were produced with vertical bonnet side louvres, these being intended for "hot weather duty" overseas. This car appears to be one of these, the louvres clearly aiding cooling of the V8.

Left: The E493A Prefect with the restyled front end, introduced early in 1949. The frontal styling was very similar to that of its bigger brother, the Pilot. There were few further changes between now and the end of the production run, the Prefect retaining the 1172 cc side-valve and transverse springing until the end. The unit-constructed 100E range superseded the Prefect.

Left: **A row of Pilots on display. The Pilot was produced between 1947 and 1951 and was the last British Ford to be powered by the side-valve V8. With the exception of the grille area sheet metal and the fact that it was a four-door, the Pilot greatly resembled the pre-war Model 62. The engine displaced 3622 cc and was coupled to a three-speed gearbox. The rest of the mechanical layout followed the usual Ford pattern of rigid axles and transverse springs. A surprising number of Pilots have survived the ravages of time, the cars now being greatly appreciated.**

CUSTOM *Fords*

World War II and after

1938 saw some new sheet-metal, mainly in the grille area, for the American models, now being designated 81A and 82A. Mechanical advances were fairly scarce but at mid-point in the year, the V8 engine got 24-stud heads instead of the earlier 21-stud versions. There were also few changes in Britain, the Model 62 being slightly altered and the 10 becoming available as a tourer.

1939 saw the restyling of the 10 once again, this time to emerge as the E93A four-door Prefect, still powered by the 1172 cc side-valve. The heritage of the redesigned front end can probably be traced back to the American Models 74 and 78 and this in turn to the 1936 Lincoln Zephyr, certain features being similar in all cases. The 8 was also superseded by a face-lifted version, this time to become the E04A Anglia, powered by the 933 cc engine. The Americans finally got hydraulic brakes, something for which Edsel had been pressing hard for years, much against his father's wishes. October 1939 saw the introduction of what came to be a perennial favourite, the "1940" Ford. Legend has it that this was the last model in which Henry Ford had a personal interest in the design, and to many came to be known as "Henry's Lady". The styling of the sedan was really an extension of the 1938 Deluxe models, however, the most significant change was, once again, in the grille area. Although there were few mechanical alterations, apart from a change to a column gear-change, the car was well received and proved to be very popular for many years after production ceased. Despite its popularity, under the skin, the transverse springs and a host of other features were getting very outdated.

It was not long before events overshadowed the regular introductions, on both sides of the Atlantic, in the form of the Second World War, with domestic car production rapidly being curtailed. The majority of the motor manufacturers' efforts were soon turned over to the war effort with military requirements clearly taking precedence.

During the war, Ford of Britain produced 360,000 military-related vehicles. This ranged from trucks and transporters to bren-gun carriers. This period also saw Ford manufacture 34,000 Rolls-Royce V12 Merlin aero engines.

The end of hostilities saw the re-introduction of a number of pre-war models in both America and Britain, with Henry Ford II taking over from his ailing grandfather.

1946 in America saw the annual restyling begin again, with eleven body styles and a choice of either a 100 horsepower V8 or a 90 horsepower six-cylinder. These models continued through until 1948 when Ford introduced their first real post-war offerings. As before, there were two series, the 98BA powered by the V8 and the 98HA powered by the six. Ford had done some serious catching-up and for the first time in its history had produced a car with independent coil front suspension. The torque-tube had been replaced by an exposed prop-shaft and the rear axle was now mounted on a pair of semi-elliptic springs. The model was good enough to pull Ford back into second place in the American market, pushing Chrysler down into third.

There were to be few luxuries for the post-war British market with a number of pre-war cars being re-introduced virtually

unaltered, bar minor detailing. The E04A Anglia was put back into production and remained there almost unchanged until the end of its life in 1948. The Prefect was also back, Dagenham's millionth vehicle being a cream Prefect driven from the line by John Wilmot, the Minister of Supply in the Attlee government.

1947 saw the death of Henry Ford, Edsel having died some years earlier. August of this year saw the appearance of a supposedly "new" British car, the Pilot. This was, in fact, very similar in many ways to the pre-war Model 62. The engine was the 3.6 litre V8, producing 85 bhp, with a 3-speed gearbox and a column-change. Unlike its American counterparts, it still retained the transverse springing. As with the rest of the range, little was done to update it, production ending in 1951. With its demise went the last V8-powered Ford of the British market.

This period saw the majority of changes limited to alterations in sheet-metal. In 1948,

the Anglia was face-lifted and given a new two-slot grille, becoming the E494A. It still retained the 933 cc engine and transverse springs, these remaining with it until the end of production in October 1953. The Prefect was also restyled and given a scaled-down version of the Pilot grill, with headlights in the wings. As with the Anglia, it still retained its old 1172 cc engine and remained virtually unaltered until its end in 1953.

The period between the late 40s and early 50s saw Ford of Britain spending a great deal of money as expansion plans were put into effect. New sites were bought, new factories built and related companies bought up. The Kelsey-Hayes Wheel Company joined the ranks, as did Briggs Motor Bodies. Ford's supply lines were now safer than ever. Despite these activities, many of the actual vehicles saw little advance until the introduction, late in 1950, of the Mark 1 Consul and Zephyr models. These showed some significant

A restoration with a difference! This beautifully restored and much adorned Fordson van seen at a Ford rally in 1986. It is an uncommon vehicle today, many having endured a hard working life in the hands of builders and farmers and so on. Mechanically, they were very similar to the passenger cars, using the same components and much of the front sheet metal. This little commercial makes an interesting and colourful addition to the vintage show scene.

changes for Ford, such as strut-type front suspension, OHV engines and an entirely new integral chassis-less construction. The Consul was powered by a four-cylinder engine of 1508 cc, giving 47 bhp, the Zephyr having a 2.3 litre straight six. The latter produced 68 bhp and necessitated a slightly longer engine bay than the Consul. If the change in mechanical parts was a complete break for Ford then the styling was even more so. The bodies had curved screens, were slab-sided and caused something of a sensation at their unveiling. The two models continued in 1952 largely as they were introduced, however, there were some interior revisions and alterations, and in the same year, both Consul and Zephyr drop-heads became available. This year also saw the introduction, by Ford of Germany, of the 15M Taunus, utilising a 1498 cc OHV engine.

1954 saw a high-performance addition to the range in the shape of the new Zodiac. This was basically a luxury edition of the Zephyr and was powered by a 71 bhp version of the straight six. The styling was clearly beginning to show a trans-Atlantic influence with two-tone paint schemes and white-wall tyres.

The Mk Is continued in production up to 1955 after which they were replaced with the Mk II range.

For those who wanted something smaller than the Consul, Zephyr or Zodiac, there was the more modestly priced unit-constructed 100E range. The four-door version was known as the Prefect and became available in October 1953. It was powered by a redesigned 1172 cc side-valve engine producing 36 bhp. The engine was based around a new casting and featured adjustable tappets. Visually, the car featured full-width body styling and a slotted grill. The front suspension was a distinct improvement over the antiquated transverse springing that the British economy models had endured for so long and consisted of an independent McPherson strut system, that had evolved from that of its larger brethren. The rear axle was now mounted on a pair of semi-elliptic leaf springs. Announced

simultaneously with the Prefect was the Anglia. This was mechanically similar and was basically a two-door version of the Prefect, although less well equipped. Later, in 1959, the Anglia became the 100E Popular.

The saloon versions were joined in 1956 by mechanically similar estate models. The Prefect version was known as the "Squire Deluxe" and the Anglia, the "Escort Estate". As with the saloons, the differences were largely cosmetic with the exception of some gearbox and rear suspension alterations.

Throughout all of this, Ford were quietly continuing to produce a car that, by any stretch of the imagination, should have no longer existed! In 1953, when Ford were busy bringing in the new Zodiac and 100E models, they also introduced the last of the "sit-up-and-beg" models, the 103E Popular. The styling and most of the major components could be traced directly back to the 30s! The car was powered by the 1172 cc side-valve, was transversely sprung and was built in the old Briggs Bodies factory in Doncaster and, remarkably, continued in production up to 1959! The only real attraction was its low price.

Meanwhile, the 100E continued in its various forms until 1959 when they were all replaced by a single model, the "Popular", which was made until 1962. Curiously, in 1960, Ford introduced the 107E, which was basically the 100E shell fitted with many of the parts from the new 105E Anglia. This model had a 997 cc ultra short-stroke OHV engine and was the first British Ford to offer a four-speed gearbox as an option. It also had a hypoid rear axle and the now familiar sloping rear window. This continued in production until 1961 and successfully paved the way for the introduction of the

Cortina range. The Anglia engines themselves went on to form the basis of Formula Three. When the 100E range finally bit the dust, around half a million side-valve powered models and 38,000 OHV 107Es had been built.

The Mk1 Consul, Zephyr, Zodiac range had been replaced in 1956 with the MkII range, introduced early in the year. These now showed very definite trans-Atlantic styling and featured a completely new six-seater body shape. Each model had its own distinctive grill and styling features. The Consul was the cheapest of the range and featured a 1073 cc four-cylinder engine. There was also a Perkins diesel-powered version available. The Zephyr and Zodiacs both had a straight six, the Zodiac, as with the Mk1s, being more extensively trimmed and hence, more expensive. Over the years, automatic transmission became available and a number of styling changes were made. Early in 1959 all three models underwent a number of alterations. This included the addition of stainless screen surrounds, and more significantly, the lowering of the roof-line. They then became known, not surprisingly, as the "Lowline" models. Production of the range ceased in 1962 when they were replaced by the MkIIIs.

For Ford of America, the post-war period

Above: **At a time when much of the British motoring public were still having to endure Ford's antiquated side-valves and transverse springs, this is what the American public were being treated to! This 1958 "Skyliner" was based on the Fairlane and is shown in the midst of its fully automatic transformation from hard-top to convertible. A complex mechanical system moves the top to the boot area when in convertible mode. It certainly makes an amazing spectacle as well as providing an interesting contrast to the British models of the time.**

really began in 1949, this being the first year of true new designs. As with Britain, the previous models had largely been carry-overs from before the war. 1950 saw what was basically 1949 models with a few modifications. There were two ranges offered, namely, the "Deluxe" and the more luxurious "Customline" designs. Engine options were a 95 bhp straight-six side-valve or a 100 bhp V8.

The next few years saw the range expanded to three main lines, namely the Mainline, Customline and Crestline. These were continued in various forms, with annual face-lifts until 1954. This year saw the end of the venerable V8, being superseded by a new 130 bhp OHV six-cylinder engine. In contrast to the British scene America saw the introduction of the infamous tail fins, culminating in the appearance of the Ford Fairlane hardtop in 1957, replacing the Crestline.

Engines available around the middle of the decade were either a 223 ci six or a 272 ci Y-block V8. The year was perhaps most noticeable for the introduction of the first of the long-running range of Thunderbirds. Ford's first entry into the "sports" car segment of the market was powered by a 292 ci version of the Y-block V8.

Facing page, bottom: **As the 1950s drew to a close, the American over-indulgences of tail-fins, chromework and gimmicks began to disappear. The styling began to become more understated and muted, although the typical American car was still a world away from what the British were driving. Slowly, the American stylists began to get away from the styles that had predominated throughout the decade. The progress of the Ford Thunderbird is interesting to follow during this period, as it gradually transformed from sports car to luxury sedan. Notice the much cleaner front end treatment of this model, a far cry from those of a few years earlier.**

A Mk I Consul and Zodiac. The range was a major breakaway from the traditional styling and featured a number of innovations. The Consul was the cheapest car of the range and was powered by a 1508 cc four-cylinder engine. The Zodiac, at the other end of the spectrum, was a high-performance version of the Zephyr Six and was powered by a six-cylinder engine of 2262 cc producing 71 bhp. The Zodiac was introduced late in 1953 and came supplied with American styling items such as two-tone paintwork and white-wall tyres. As is clearly illustrated, the front end styling differed between models.

1956 saw the previous year's models face-lifted, with the restyled Thunderbird being offered with a selection of three V8s, each with a different power output. There were also three additions to the Fairlane range.

The oil crisis of the same year hit the car and oil companies hard and economy became the name of the game. To this end, Ford launched the Falcon in Europe.

A Mk II Zephyr being lovingly prepared for a rally. The Zephyr, as well as the Zodiac, was powered by a six-cylinder engine, clearly giving better performance than the lowly Consul's four. Each of the models of the range had different front end styling in the form of grille and sheet metal This particular Zephyr is clearly in excellent condition!

A further example of a Mk II Zephyr convertible, looking better than new. These cars were the ultimate "cruiser" of the post-war period and retained their popularity long after they were phased out of production. They are clearly not without their fans today!

Facing page, top: **A line-up of Mk II Consuls on display. The Consul was introduced early in 1956 and, as with the Mk Is, was the cheapest of the range, powered by a 1703 cc four-cylinder. It was also the plainest model, with a simple grille and no over-riders. The Consul was frequently updated by the addition of two-tone paint and white-walls, in order to emulate its upmarket brother, the Zodiac.**

It was in 1959 that, in Britain, Costain and Duckworth, who had set up a tuning firm, started to get to grips with the 997 cc Anglia engine. They made it a Formula Junior winner and supplied Lotus cars with race-prepared Anglia engines. These engines were named after their effective creators, "Cosworth".

The Cosworths were running at Brands Hatch by December 1959 and finally achieved success with Jim Clark winning at Goodwood in a Cosworth powered Lotus, producing over 90 bhp. He later managed a second in a Lotus Ford at Indianapolis.

The Sixties onwards

Another firm to take advantage of Fords new creation was the Ginetta Car Company who, in the early 60s, used the Anglia 105E engine as their standard. As an option, the 1340 cc Classic engine was available for about £16 extra. The same period saw the arrival of the Leaf Lynx Roadster, which was based on Zephyr components.

The Cortina was next off the production line and was available with varying trim and engine options, including a 1500 cc GT version, complete with Weber carburettor. Jackie Stewart's American racing debut was in such a car. At the same time, a Lotus Cortina was introduced, powered by a twin overhead cam engine which proved very successful in rally circles and subsequently formed the basis for Fords attack on Grand Prix racing.

The years that followed saw the Classic,

The 105E Anglia represented another break with tradition for Ford, being fitted with the new 997 cc OHV engine, four-speed gearbox and McPherson front suspension. A 1200 cc powered version later joined the ranks. The sloping rear window caused much comment at the time although it soon became accepted. This trio shows an interesting selection of styles. On the left is a much-modified circuit-styled version, in the centre, a fully restored example and on the right, a rally-orientated car. In its day, the little 105E was well represented in many forms of motor sport as well as commonplace on the streets.

Classic Capri and Corsair, improve in looks and specification whilst the Cortina became a Mk II with a range that included Base, Deluxe, Super, Estates, E and GT. A notable variant of the Cortina range was a special, V6 powered, high-performance version built by Jeoff Uren of Savage fame. Consul, Zephyr, Zodiac and Executive Mk IIIs and IVs were now around and by the late 60s many other manufacturers were beginning to notice the popularity of these, and other models and use Ford components in their own vehicles. Examples of this included Cobra, HRG, TVR and Sunbeam. The Cobra was the brainchild of Carroll Shelby, winner of Le Mans in 1959, whose dream was to create his own sports car. In 1961 he came up with the idea of dropping the new 4.3 litre Ford V8 into the AC chassis, thus creating the legendary Cobra. Initially, in 1962, the car was built at Thames Ditton and fitted with a 4.7 litre Ford V8. It went on to achieve great success on both sides of the Atlantic. Never content, Shelby went on to produce highly tuned Mustangs and also became heavily involved with the GT40 programme.

By 1965 HRG had built a space-framed two-seater sports car which used a Ford Cortina engine and a number of other rolling components. TVR brought out a

small sports car, called the Griffith, which used a Ford Fairlane V8 engine producing 271 bhp, giving a top speed in excess of 145 mph. Later in the year, Sunbeam also got in on the act with a Ford V8-powered Alpine called the Tiger.

The Escort was introduced in 1967, initially as a small family car, with the usual

This is the view that most people got – the rear end of a Mk II Cortina Savage. This particular car was painstakingly rebuilt by Mike Birch over a number of years and is a Mk II series I, built by Savages in 1968. It is especially unusual as it is a 3000 E four-door and one of the few surviving overdrive models. Ford's 3-litre Essex V6 provided the power for these rapid cars, top speed being in the region of 120 mph.

The much loved Mk I Cortina was available in a number of forms with a wide range of engine and trim options. The Cortina was represented in a variety of motoring activities, from rallying to drag racing, with tens of thousands of others on the streets. It was an immensely popular car and formed the basis of cheap daily transport for a large percentage of the motoring population. Although now fewer in number, many, such as this pristine example, are being cared for by enthusiasts.

CUSTOM *Fords*

trim ranges. By this time the Mk I and II Lotus Cortina's were having trouble keeping up with the opposition in rallies, so Ford decided to put the Lotus-Ford twin-cam into the Escort body. The engine wouldn't fit, so was put in askew in order to squeeze it in! This was carried out at Halewood with all of the twin-cam models being two-door versions, white in colour and sporting four quarter-bumpers. The car was first raced by Roger Clarke who

Above: An example of a 1968 Mustang, one of the many variants that Ford of America produced over a long period. The Mustang was regularly restyled and re-equipped, resulting in a wide range of cars. This, coupled with the variety of engine options offered, gave rise to a large number of possible combinations, a choice not often available to the average British motorist of the period.

Nowadays becoming a fairly scarce car. This is a V4 powered Corsair, here in the form of an immaculate Crayford convertible. The convertibles have always been few and far between, and are now catered for by an enthusiastic owners' club. Crayford also carried out their soft-top conversions on a number of other Ford models.

Below: A selection of specials. On the left is a 1600E Mk II Cortina. Centre stage is a Mk I Lotus Cortina and to the right is a Mk II Crayford Cortina. All three models are still favoured by enthusiasts and have their appropriate owners' clubs. Surviving cars of all three types are now well cared for.

won the 1968 Scottish Rally in a special 152 bhp version. The development continued and the Escort range was increased to include E and GT versions as well as an Escort Mexico, the latter named after a rallying triumph. By 1968 Fords had introduced, onto the British scene, its first purpose-built sporty coupe, the Capri. There was a Capri from the early 60s but this was merely a coupe version of the Classic. The new Capri range had a choice of trim levels and could be purchased with a choice of four engine sizes namely, 1300, 1600, 2000 and 3000 cc. The power output ranged from 57 bhp with the 1300, to 136 bhp for the 3000 which was good for 115 mph. The Capris were facelifted but remained essentially unchanged until 1974 when a Mk II hatchback was introduced. This was instantly a great success as no other British firm produced anything like it. Plenty of tuning equipment was available, with various Ford engines being fitted, up to V6. The Capri was also entered in the Super Saloon Car Championship and competed very well with a DFV Formula 1 unit giving over 180 mph.

Front-wheel drive arrives

The early 70s also saw the development of Fords first small, front-wheel drive car, the Fiesta. This started on the drawing board as the Bobcat and a number of prototypes were developed. By this time fuel economy had taken priority over performance. The engines were initially chosen as 35 bhp, later to become 40 and 52 bhp versions having cubic capacities of 957 and 1117 cc respectively. It was decided that all the models would have three doors and that the range would consist of Base, L, S and Ghia. The S had stiffer suspension, with rear anti-roll bar and the Ghia came with woodgrain trim, headrests and velour upholstery. A Ghia model was introduced as, in 1970, the Ford Motor Company bought 80% of Ghia's shares and by 1972 owned the entire company. Ghia's first project was a small sports car called the Corrida which was based on the 1117 cc Fiesta. The mid 70s saw improvements in the Fiesta range with the introduction of the Sports models and low or high compression options for the 957 cc models range.

The mid 70s also saw the introduction of the Mk II Escort. Trim for the new range was as usual, from Basic Popular to the Ghia. In addition, a 1600 Sport model was brought out, together with Rally Sport (RS) 1800 and 2000 versions. Many parts were becoming available by now and body-kits for RS cars were becoming commonplace. The RS 2000 was the most popular and was available as a two-door, four-seater with a four-cylinder 1993 cc engine producing, in standard form, 110 bhp with a maximum speed of over 110 mph. The Escort, in its Mk II form continued up to 1979 when various special editions, such as the Capital, Harrier and Goldcrest, were released.

1974 was the year that the Mk IV Zephyrs left the scene and were replaced by 3.0 litre Essex versions of the Granada and Consul range. These had a power output of 140 bhp and a maximum speed of 115 mph. Many trims were available, the top of the range being the Ghia 3000 with automatic transmission as standard. The launch of this large luxury car coincided with the launch, in the States, of the 1.5 ton Mercury Monarch, which was powered by either a straight 6 or V8. So Britain and the US were gradually beginning to forget about economy and return to performance but this time with added luxury as well.

By 1977 a new Granada was launched with, 2.0, 2.3, and 2.8 litre models. There was also a diesel 2.0L version powered by a Peugeot engine and a new 2.8 V6 engine (with fuel injection) powering the 2.8S. Similar power-plants up to 2.3 litre were also made available for the Cortina range. The new Cortina Ghias, at that time, came supplied with 1.6S uprated Capri engines.

1978 arrived and brought with it the start of numerous special editions to tempt prospective purchasers, in a total market which was, due to the recession, falling. The Fiesta started the specials with a Kingfisher and Anniversary, both based on the 1100L model. This coincided with the launch of the series III Capri which to all intents and purposes was the same as the series II except for the front spoiler, new redesigned grill and wrap-around bumpers. The Granada range was reduced following the introduction of the 2.8i GLS saloon and estate which replaced the 2.8iS and GL, and sported low-profile TRX tyres.

1979 started with another Fiesta special, this time called the Sandpiper and again based on the 1100 cc model but with bronze/beige, or just bronze bodywork. By the end of the year an 1100GL and 1300GL had been added to the Fiesta range. As far as the Cortina was concerned, this year saw some minor body restyling and although still the Mk IV, in some circles it was referred to as the Mk V. The Cortina S was discontinued but an S pack option was made available. A pick-up, the P100, was also launched, based on the Mk V Cortina, it sold particularly well toward the end of 1979. The year ended with Granada automatics being launched and a special edition Granada Sapphire arriving on the scene.

1980 was a busy year for Ford as they redesigned one of their most popular cars, the Escort. Engine options of 1.1, 1.3 and 1.6 litre were available. All were either three of five-door models with a trim range from Popular to Ghia. All the Escorts (1.3 & 1.6) had the new cylindrical valve head engines (CVH) with aluminium cylinder heads and all were front-wheel drive. Later in the year, estate versions and the XR3 were launched. The latter had a specially tuned 1596 cc engine with twin-choke carburettor and gas dampers. Ventilated front disc-brakes were standard, together with low-profile tyres and a distinctive rear spoiler. The other models in the Ford range had minor changes. The Capri had a GL added to its ranks and the Granada a 2.3 Ghia. There were new additions to the Fiesta range in the shape of the Firefly and Festival, based on the 950 and 1100L. Towards the end of the year a Fiesta 950GL and 950/1100 Popular and Popular Plus became available, the Popular having

An example of, perhaps, one of the most rapid standard production vehicles ever to become available to the British motorist, the RS 2000. These rally-bred cars were capable of out-handling and performing far more expensive sports cars. Not surprisingly, many were put to use in a variety of forms of motor sport, however, even in unmodified form, they made a very rapid road car. a number of variations were produced, some powered by twin-cam engines. They are still fast cars, even by today's standards.

A typical American Ford product of the 1980s. This Turbo Mustang reflects the dramatic alterations in American styling that have occurred over the last decade. Although the European influence is evident the distinctive American "look" is still present.

definite "budget" specification. During the following two years, a Fiesta Supersport, based on a 1300S, with light alloy wheels arrived, together with Bravo 1100 and 1300 models. December 1981 saw the sporty XR2 hatchback launched. This used the Fiesta body with the addition of extended wheel arches, rear spoilers, deep section bumpers, and a 1598 cc OHV engine.

Around the same time, the Escort range saw the introduction of five-speed gearboxes, this helping to improve fuel economy. By 1982, the XR3 had been replaced by the XR3i which was powered by a 1597 cc engine. RS1600i versions were available on special order. The sporty image was continued with the introduction of the Capri LS (replacing the 1.6S) and the 2.8i Capri injection, based on a 2793 cc engine with electronic fuel injection. A 1.6 Cabaret Capri was launched and followed by Cabaret II versions of the 1.6 and 2.0 models. The 2.8i was also improved by the addition of Recaro seats and tinted glass. The Granadas continued the trend of specials with the Granada Consort 2.0L and 2.3L. Minor revisions to all of the Granada models soon followed.

Aerodynamics and high-technology

The Cortina had carried on successfully, over the years clocking up record sales and in 1981 and 1982 Carousel and Crusader models were added to the range. The end of 1982 arrived and Ford took their biggest gamble, the launch of the Cortina's replacement, the Sierra. Months of speculation were over. Whereas most other manufacturers tended to favour front-wheel drive (even in their large cars) Ford stuck with conventional rear-wheel drive for the Sierra. The new aerodynamic design came as a shock to a lot of people and was initially referred to as a "jelly mould" in some quarters! Consequently the initial sales were poor, but things gradually picked up and figures later in the following year saw the Sierra riding high on the "cars sold" lists. All the models were hatchbacks with estates later being made available. The range was from a 1.3 to a 2.3 litre with a 2.3 litre diesel variant. The 1.3 had a Taunus engine and a four-speed gearbox. The 1.6 and 2.0 had similar engines to the old Cortina range, with four-speed gearboxes, although a five-speed was an option. The 2.3 had the 2294 V6 whereas the 2.3D had the 2304 cc Peugeot diesel and a five-speed gearbox. The car also had a new independent suspension and front and rear anti-roll bars. 1983 saw the arrival of the XR4i, a three-door Sierra hatchback, with an uprated V6 2792 cc fuel injected engine. It came with a five-speed gearbox as standard and sported a characteristic bi-plane rear spoiler. Later in the year, economy versions of the Sierra were introduced.

During the blaze of publicity surrounding the Sierra launch, some of the other models also saw improvements. The Fiesta Quartz and Finesse hit the streets together with new economy versions of the 950 and 1100. The end of 1983 also saw a redesign of the complete Fiesta range. The main differences were cosmetic, sloping bonnets, small grills, integral spoilers etc. The usual model trims and power plants were available and a new 1600 Fiesta diesel, Popular Plus and L were launched in early 1984. The XR2 was also uprated, now having the Escort-like 1597 CVH engine.

The end of 1983 saw the demise of most of the Capri range with only the 1.6LS, 2.0S and 2.8i being retained. This coincided with the launch of 1.3, 1.6 and 1.6i cabriolet Escorts. The two-door body had a lined hood with heated rear screen and alloy wheels. At this time, the Orion was launched, this being basically an Escort with a boot. The first Orions were only available as GL or Ghia models however, the range was later increased to include a 1.6i, which was similar to the XR3i. 1984 saw the launch of 1.3 and 1.6L Orion models and

A heavily adorned XR2 Fiesta. This particular car sports various alterations not, in this case, merely for effect. This is a Goodliff Racing Fiesta, driven by Barry "Whizzo" Williams in the Fiesta Credit Championship. For this form of competition, the engine/gearbox must remain unmodified, however, suspension alterations are permitted to upgrade the handling.

was also a good year for Laser special editions of other models. These included 1.6 and 2.0 Capris, 1.3 and 1.6 Sierras and later in the following year, an Escort Laser. The Granada had 2.0LX and 2.3LX saloons and estates added to the range with special 2.8, 2.8i Ghia and Executive editions.

The Granada was redesigned in 1985 and appeared as a five-door hatchback. 1.8, 2.0 and 2.0i versions were available as L, GL and Ghia versions. The 2.8i and Scorpio topped the range, the latter having air-conditioning and electrically adjustable front seats. All had a five-speed gearbox and the option of four-speed A4LD lock-up automatic transmission. Later in the year, the 2.8i Ghia and Scorpio 4x4 were launched. The power of these four-wheel drive cars, developed by the Special Vehicle Engineering Team, was divided on a 34:66 basis. They also came equipped with an anti-lock braking system.

1986 saw the Escort and Orion ranges restyled in a similar cosmetic manner to the Fiesta range. They became the first "small cars" to have an anti-lock braking system as an option. Economy being the name of the game led to the introduction of a new 1.4 litre lean-burn CVH engine which was available in Fiestas, Escorts and Orions. A new sporty 1.4S Fiesta, loosely based on the XR2, was also launched. Economy versions of the Sierra appeared, all 1.6 models with the E-Max economy engine. Things did get a little more performance orientated, as in May 1986, the new 2.0 Efi Sierra (capable of 0-60 in around 9 seconds) joined the group, together with an XR4x4i and a 1.8S and LX. The power ratios of the XR4x4 were split as with the Granada. The Capri got into the act with a 2.8i Special, with a 0-60 time of around 7.9 seconds. A 200 bhp, Turbo Technics, turbocharged version of the 2.8i Capri was made available through the main dealers at an additional cost of £1300 and an optional extra, much needed, was an advanced braking kit.

May 21st 1986 saw a white Transit van leave the production line. Not an unusual occurrence except that this was the 20 millionth Ford built in Britain. Whilst on production figures, 1986 saw the Escort

approach 5,000,000 sales world-wide. The small car was popular in the States although the US versions came with an excess of chrome which many said detracted from the clean lines of the European version. The new 1986 American version of the XR3 was better in this respect. The chrome had gone and power was provided by a 1.9 litre CVH engine which incidently, due to pollution control etc, was only 3 bhp better than the British 1.6i. In the States, the XR was known as the Ford Escort GT. Although American Escorts looked similar they were, in fact vastly different from the European versions. The body shells were different and panel and running gear alterations meant that parts were not interchangeable between the two versions. Mercury also produced the Escort XR3 but called it the Lynx, this being the flagship of the range. One addition to the American market was the EXP, a coupe of sorts, with a similar line to the British Capri. A stable-mate for the EXP was the LN7 which featured a large "bubble back" glass hatch.

1986 was also a good year for Ford Motor Sport. Andy Rouse, three times RAC British Saloon Car Champion followed his 1985 win in his 2.3 litre Group A Sierra XR4x4Ti with continued successes in 1986.

The mid-engined RS 200 was launched, mainly for rallying, and was powered by an all-aluminium four-cylinder engine based on the Cosworth BDA unit. The engine had a capacity of 1.8 litres and was turbocharged. It produced 230 bhp and gave a 0-60 time of about five seconds but for competition use, the power could be tweaked to 380 bhp. It was rear-wheel or four-wheel drive (37:63), the option being driver selectable. It was, in 1986, doing very well in rallies and in particular going great guns for Stig Blomquist in the Swedish Hillclimb Championship.

For a few years Ford's famous dominance of Grand Prix racing had lapsed, until 1986 saw the arrival of a new turbocharged 1.5 litre V6 Ford engine designed by Ford and Cosworth Engineering of Northampton. The new V6 Ford Formula 1 engine had twin turbochargers plus a sophisticated electronic engine management system using a Ford EEC-1V on-board computer. This was developed by Ford's electrical and electronic engineering division and programmed jointly by Ford and Cosworth. The system continually monitored the engine, ignition and turbocharger and was also capable of self diagnosis. A spin-off from this combination was the new Sierra RS Cosworth which was designed to be the spearhead of Ford's rally programme in 1987. The car had a maximum speed of 150 mph and a 0-60 time of 6.5 seconds. Electronically controlled anti-lock four-wheel disc brakes (ABS) were fitted as standard equipment. The new Cosworth was fitted with twin overhead camshafts, alloy cylinder head with 16 valves, a Garrett Air Research T3 turbocharger and a Weber/Marelli multipoint fuel injection and electronic engine management system. Racing versions of the Sierra may well be used in the proposed World Touring Car Championship early in 1987.

The end of 1986 saw a lot of outside firms getting more interested in Ford's new engines. Scimitar continued production of their SS1 sports car using 1.3 and 1.6 Escort CVH engines. Panther started utilising a Ford five-speed gearbox with 2.8 V6 power. The AC Ace made a comeback with a new handcrafted aluminium 2 + 2 body, a

This is an example of the Sierra five-door XR8, bred at Ford South Africa. Power is provided by a North American Mustang 5-litre V8 (Cleveland 302, producing 225 bhp), fitted with a Holley 4V carburettor and a five-speed gearbox. Other additions include ventilated discs, uprated suspension, tyres and running gear. The performance figures are very impressive with a 0-60 time of 6 seconds and a top speed of around 145 mph, although this does lead to fuel figures of about 24 mpg. Ford of South Africa also produce a Sierra XR6 which contains the 3-litre Essex engine, the South African answer to the XR4x4i.

Ford Sierra 2.8 litre engine, XR4x4 four-wheel drive system, five-speed gearbox and the anti-lock braking system.

CUSTOM *Fords*

The end of 1986 saw the introduction of an Escort RS turbo and an Escort RS turbo with custom pack.

As for the future, one can only guess, but perhaps a few clues can be had from the 1986 Turin Show. Ghia's Probe V was resplendent in a new red coat, as was the Ghia Vignale TSX-6, an American Ford Tempo estate but offering oh-so-much room! This was a six-seater with the third row of passengers sitting slightly higher than the row in front. This gave better visibility and that "riding in a coach" feeling. The middle and rear seats all folded down and with the tailgate out of the way and the roof unclipped formed a giant "pick-up". The instrumentation was, of course, fully electronic. Is this the shape of things to come? With a company as large and diverse as Ford we can only guess.

CHAPTER TWO

Custom Fords and their origins

Speedsters and Dirt-tracks

From its conception until the emergence of Henry Ford as the champion of mass production, the motor car was largely the plaything of the rich. At the turn of the century, the average person still regarded these strange-looking, noisy machines with a mixture of awe, mistrust and reverence. For some years this continued to be the normal state of affairs, however, when Henry Ford's first mass-produced offering, the Model T, became available to all and sundry, attitudes changed dramatically.

For a few years after its introduction, the Model T was still largely in the hands of the comparatively well-off, As the numbers on the streets rose and the price decreased as Ford's assembly line techniques became established, so more and more people got their hands on their first car. For the younger element, it was almost inevitably a well-worn and often battered Model T, still the only car to fall within their limited fiscal grasp. More often than not, it would be a roadster as these were generally cheaper still.

After the initial excitement had worn off

Above:
This immaculate early Roadster has a number of period pieces such as "tear-drop" lights and Halibrand "quick-change" axle centre section. Various forms of the latter are still being produced by a number of American manufacturers. They enable the rear-end ratio to be changed in a matter of minutes. Because of the high cost, these are uncommon on British Rods.

and the T's shortcomings, especially in terms of performance, had been exposed, the quest for more speed and power soon took hold. As Henry Ford often argued, improved performance was easier and cheaper to achieve by means of weight reduction rather than increased

horse-power. This was undeniably correct, the main problem being that there were few inessential frills and creature comforts that could be stripped from the Model T in order to lighten it. The result was that "essential" parts began to be lost as cars were robbed of their hoods, bumpers, wings, windshields and running-boards. Anything that could be taken off to reduce the weight was removed and discarded. The first stripped-down "speedsters" had arrived.

Perhaps the nearest thing to a 1930s Lakes car. This Special was based on Model B running gear, with an early 21-stud flathead V8 and an open sports body. The car was found in derelict condition in Gloucestershire and is being systematically restored to its former glory. Similarly based cars could be seen throughout the 1930s and 1940s at various British motoring events such as hill climbs and trials.

CUSTOM *fords*

The T was a light car, so with much of its bodywork disposed of, quite respectable performance, for the era, could be achieved. Admittedly, this was often at the expense of comfort and weather protection. However, as much of this early action was taking place in sunny California and youngsters tend to be rather hardier than their parents, the latter may well have been of minimal significance!

The next stage in their development was by the rudimentary tuning of the T's four-cylinder side-valve, the performance of which was hampered by a number of constraints not least of all, restricted breathing. Early attempts to overcome this consisted of simple tubular manifolds or additional carburettors simply welded to modified standard items. Open exhausts were mandatory, the crackle of which helped to further raise the eye-brows of many, already suspicious, civil and police authorities. Apart from skimming the head, there was little else that could be done to increase the performance. If automobile engineering was still in its infancy, performance tuning was even more so.

Within a few years it became apparent that there was sufficient interest in these increasingly popular speedsters to support several companies who were beginning to specialise in the manufacture and fitting of tuning and performance-related parts. This era saw the emergence of manufacturers whose names were to go down in the annals of hot-rodding history. Companies such as Rajo and Riley began producing numerous hot-up parts such as cams, manifolds, exhaust systems and cylinder heads. Numerous conversion kits arrived on the scene, capable of converting the side-valve T engine to an overhead set-up or even a double overhead cam arrangement.

This was an era of great ingenuity, often born of necessity, perhaps nowhere more so than in the area of carburation. Apart from commercially available parts, it was still fairly common to find intake systems and multiple carburettors taken from such diverse sources as boats, motorcycles and aircraft! Although many were grossly inefficient in terms of economy, they generally showed some improvement over the standard items. By contemporary standards, the power output from even a well-tuned T engine was small, although, when coupled to a lightweight, stripped roadster, devoid of all frills, surprisingly good performance could be achieved.

Henry Ford's thoughts concerning this tampering with his beloved Model T have not been recorded, but one suspects that, although, in later years he turned away from racing, he may well have had a sneaking approval. After all, if his "Arrow" and "999" racers were not hot-rods, then nothing was! He could possibly be regarded as one of the first innovative, ingenious "back yard" hot-rodders that were to become so prevalent in later years.

Following the demise of the Model T in 1927, the Model A made its debut. Its introduction had two effects on the early hot-rodding fraternity. Initially, it made the already cheap and plentiful Model T even

cheaper, as people changed their old "Tin Lizzies" for the stylish new As. It also heralded the arrival of the "new and improved" four-cylinder side-valve engine with nearly double the power output of its predecessor. This resulted in a new flurry of activity as manufacturers tooled-up to produce hot-up parts for the new engine. More conversion heads became available as companies such as McDowell and Cragar began to offer overhead valve and overhead cam conversions. Cars got noticeably faster!

Dirt-track racing continued its popularity with cars getting more specialised and better built. When, in 1932, the Model B four-cylinder engine arrived, it was immediately pounced on and put to good use (as was the more famous V8). As previously, overhead valve and overhead cam conversion heads were often added, resulting in an appreciable increase in horsepower.

Typical, if there was such a thing, half mile dirt track racers of the period used either Model T or 27/28 Chevrolet chassis, sometimes narrowed and often fitted with 1927 T bodies. Ford front axles and transverse springs were used, as were early V8 axles, sometimes fitted with a Halibrand "quick change" centre section.

CUSTOM *Fords*

Below:
This is how hot-rods looked in the "good old days" but they were rarely built as well as this example. The car was put together by Bernie Chodosh using a 1932 chassis with most of the running gear coming from an assortment of 1940 Fords. The engine is a 24-stud side-valve of 1942 vintage, bored out to 239 ci and fitted with many vintage tuning parts. This includes Offenhauser high compression heads, Thickstun inlet and Stromberg 97 carburettors. This period piece sees plenty of active use, including drag-strip events .

Facing page, Bottom:
This re-creation of an early Lakes-style Roadster was built by Brian Lucas using a 1932 chassis with an imported American fibre-glass Roadster body. A 1946 Ford supplied the back axle, shocks, brakes and a number of other parts. The chassis was heavily reworked and now includes a Model A front cross-member to lower the car further. The engine is a 24-stud 239 ci Mercury 59A unit, fitted with Edelbrock heads and fed by triple carburettors on an Offenhauser inlet manifold. A classic piece!

This enabled racers to change the rear axle ratio in a matter of minutes to suit the particular track and conditions. Power was provided by either a tuned A, or more likely a B engine, suitably hotted-up by the addition of a conversion head, cam and open exhaust system. Wheels were generally of the 15'' or 16'' quick-change variety.

Similar racers/rods could be seen on many of the American dirt tracks right through the 30s and 40s. Fast as these four-cylinder powered cars were, they couldn't hold a candle to their big brother, the V8.

The V8

If there is a single engine that could be described as *the* hot-rodders engine, it must undeniably be Henry Ford's side-valve V8. Introduced in 1932, it rapidly assumed a position of major importance in various forms of motoring activity across the world. The first engines produced around 65 bhp and when dropped into a lightweight roadster body, produced performance and speed that was unheard of except with expensive, up-market cars. As if this wasn't enough, each year seemed to bring more horsepower from the factory. 1933 saw the introduction of higher compression aluminium heads. 1934 saw better carburation in the form of the new Stromberg 48 and a power increase to 85 bhp while 1937 brought a new crankshaft and bigger main journals. 1939 heralded the introduction of the Mercury car line with further improvements to the engine, notably an increase in bore size.

The V8 continued throughout the next decade and in 1949, the Mercury's stroke was increased, resulting in a displacement of 255.4 cubic inches. This engine continued in production up to 1953 and was known as the 8BA unit. It was an engine that rodders and racers went for, if they could get their hands on one, but perhaps we are getting a little ahead of ourselves here.

Following its introduction in 1932, it was only a matter of time before V8s began to appear in breakers-yards. Once this happened, it didn't take long for them to

The power-plant of this re-creation of an early rod features a side-valve V8 with twin carburettors, SCOT blower and Harrell high compression heads. Attention to detail and a high degree of engineering differentiates it from its predecessors. Other period features include early wire wheels. Built by Simon Lane, the car, despite the lack of top and wings, sees plenty of use throughout the year.

find their way into the hands of the "speed-crazy" youngsters. Even a well tuned four-cylinder was no match for the new V8 "flat-head", as it soon came to be known. A stripped-down roadster with 85 bhp or more on tap was a match for anything but the most exotic cars. This was the ultimate rodder's fantasy, to take on fast, "sports" cars and to beat them with a cheap, home-built car created with his own hands.

As the V8-powered Model 18 began to find its way around the world as a result of Ford's many overseas plants and connections, it began to make inroads into other spheres of motor sport. The cars set speed records at a number of venues in Europe and Britain, doing well on the three mile banked concrete track at Brooklands, once again breaking records.

There were some similarities between Brooklands racers of the period and the American cars as both encouraged the use of lightweight roadster/tourer bodies as well as the removal of various pieces of bodywork in order to lighten and streamline them. Model 18s also set records on the 7.8 mile Montlhery banked circuit, fifteen miles from Paris. Numerous record attempts were made here as there were no noise regulations, as at Brooklands, so cars could run throughout the night.

As a result of its excellent performance, the car fulfilled the sporting aspirations of many amateur sportsman drivers and was driven to great success in sprints, such as the Brighton standing quarter kilometre, attracting much public attention. Others were driven in road trials and also did well at hill-climbs, such as Shelsey Walsh and Prescott. Unlike the racing activity now developing in America, the majority of modified cars were run at various forms of "organised" motor sport. British "specials" seem to have rarely indulged in the equivalent of the American street-racing. Most appear to have been content to limit their activities to the race-track!

The Lakes

America, in the 1930s, saw another indigenous form of racing appear and develop, a form which was really without parallel. This was largely due to the topography of the particular region of southern California that hosted it. High in the desert area across the mountains from Los Angeles were a number of dry lake beds. These were extremely dusty but very smooth and hard, making ideal proving grounds for hot-rodders. Initially, the lakes echoed to the sound of a few Model T and A roadsters as use was made of these vast expanses, but before long, their usefulness was spread by word of mouth and numbers began to rocket. Soon, it was not unusual to see several hundred Ford roadsters turn up each weekend and indulge in, sometimes chaotic, high speed racing. Some of the cars were not well constructed. Tales abound of cars lacking floor boards, brackets and chassis tack welded together and engine mounts fashioned from chunks of wood. It seems that nostalgia has dimmed many a memory!

At the time, the only interest was in performance, with looks and safety coming well down the list of priorities. The streets crackled to the sound of unmuffled motors as dust-covered early Fords were used as daily transport and weekend racers by hundreds of young Californians. Many of the cars were never cleaned, let alone repainted or chromed, the owners preferring to "wear" their dust throughout the week. Filters might be cleaned, oil changed and bearings repacked, but polish the paintwork? Never!

Clearly things had reached a stage where an organising body was needed and this, following the fusion of several clubs, emerged as the Southern California Timing Association (SCTA). Civil authorities were more than happy with the situation as it helped to reduce the problem of street-racing. The racers were also happy as it meant that they could test their cars to the limit in comparative safety. Some abandoned dirt-track racing as the lakes offered far less chance of damage, especially to the car's bodywork.

As time passed, speeds increased and the future for lakes racing seemed assured. Roadsters began to emerge with peculiar wind-cheating bodies and if possible, stripped-down even further. Throughout all this ran the common thread of Ford Model Ts, As and the occasional B/18. The engines were a mixture of T, A and B four-cylinders and latterly, the much-loved V8. Gradually a greater variety of engines and marques began to appear but the sport of lakes racing owes much of its heritage to these dusty often rough, but fast Ford roadsters of yesteryear.

The lakes have left their mark on today's street-driven rods in the shape of heavily chopped tops, streamlined noses and, of course, a lack of running boards, wings etc. Many of the current "clean" lines of contemporary street-rods are a direct result of the attempts to streamline and lighten the early boxy roadsters, coupes and sedans.

With the arrival of the Second World War, many things temporarily came to a halt for the duration of the hostilities. Lakes racing was no exception. Many of the avid young rodder/racers were sent off to war and their cars left stored or abandoned. The lakes later became unavailable, as before long, they had been permanently closed and taken over by the US Air Force for aircraft and weapons testing.

After the war, only El Mirage was left open, with the SCTA back in action and the same pre-war roadsters, now turning in speeds in excess of 150 mph. With the coming of the 50s and the advent of legalized drag racing, many SoCal rodders finally abandoned the lakes. Numbers gradually dwindled as the more accessible drag-strips were adopted.

Remarkably, El Mirage still hosts a monthly meeting for the die-hards, although numbers are now rarely in excess of one hundred entries. Many of the cars still racing are the many-times rebuilt Ford roadsters and coupes from generations before.

Although the numbers participating has dwindled over the years, there is still considerable prestige attached to this form of motor sport. In 1981, Ford's Lincoln-Mercury division took two specially built cars to Lake Bonneville, in Utah, with the intention of smashing a number of long-standing land speed records. Their involvement is not so surprising when one remembers Henry Ford's opinion that "Racers sell stockers". The one car was a full streamliner and the other an LN 7, both powered by various Mercury CVH engines. The liner ran 262 mph and the LN 7 established records in twelve national and ten international classes. Even today, this almost archaic form of motor sport still has influence and relevance to some of the styles and techniques currently being applied to a wide spectrum of vehicles.

Early Customs

Around the late 30s to early 40s, when all the racing action was taking place at the dry lakes, another peculiar motoring phenomenon was coming into being. The newer Fords, when compared to the boxy Ts, As and Bs, were much more bulbous and rounded, reflecting the predominant styles of the times. These cars, being newer, obviously cost considerably more than the rock-bottom priced roadsters, the owners tending to be rather older and financially better off than the roadster group. Whereas the youngsters in their stripped, hotted-up roadsters had absolutely no interest in the appearance of their cars, with the new group, the looks and style were of paramount importance, performance coming second. The newer cars were completely different from the earlier Fords. For instance, there was no practical way that they could be stripped down. Their wings in particular, formed an integral part of the flowing, more streamlined lines that were now emerging from Ford's stylists. There was no way that the older ideas could readily be adapted to the newer styles. Despite the fact that the later models came readily equipped with the V8, performance was of less importance than the visual aspect. The bodywork of the cars often came in for considerable modification resulting in the first "true customs".

The idea behind customising was to make the lines of the car even more "aerodynamic" than the standard factory offerings. Ideally it would be altered sufficiently to hide its true identity and origins. The cars were lowered as far as practicable and the rear wheel openings covered with "fender skirts", almost completely masking the wheels. All unnecessary chrome trim, ornaments, door handles, badges and accessories were removed and the resultant holes and seams filled with lead to clean up and further smooth out the body lines. Running boards were generally discarded and grilles and bumpers changed. Late 30s De Soto bumpers were highly prized items. The wheels were invariably covered by custom discs and fitted with wide white-wall tyres. The most major modification of many Fords of this period, was a top chop. This entailed cutting off the entire roof, taking out several inches or more from the door pillars and rewelding the roof back into place at the lower level. The bodywork involved in such an operation was extensive, as were the skills of the body-man required to perform the task. The result, when successful was a sleek, tear-drop shape with no sharp or sudden changes in lines, everything flowing gently towards the rear. If a convertible formed the basis of the project, the screen and surround were chopped and a solid "convertible" top (known as a Carson top) fitted. The interiors were almost universally white.

The most popular cars for this treatment were 1935-1941 Fords and 1939-1940 Mercuries, many looking very similar after the treatment. The end result was usually treated to a single colour paint scheme to further enhance the car's new, smoother lines. These styles continued up to the outbreak of World War II. The war put an end to any advancement of this, as with many other, automotive trends. After the war things once again picked up where they had left off, the 1948-51 Fords and Mercuries being particularly popular.

It's ironic how attempts to personalise a car and make it unique often result in a set of "rules" governing what is and what is not acceptable. With early hot rods these "rules" resulted in hundreds of similar looking T and A roadsters, often V8-powered. Similarly, many customs ended up looking like one another, only differing in minor details.

CUSTOM Fords

Post-war customising

The post-war trend produced more variation and the single, dark-coloured paint schemes gave way to flames, two-tones, scallops and trick paint finishes. Body modifications also began to get more radical.

Following the end of World War II and the "escape" from the armed services by thousands of young men, the custom craze began to build up rapidly. They began to look for new stylish cars to buy, the problem being that new cars were still a rarity. As a result, they turned their attention to the sleekest of the pre-war offerings, mainly the V8-powered 1939, 1940 and 1941 Fords. These cars were reworked in order to give them the "aerodynamic" look, as with the pre-war customs, but perhaps even more so. Many hundreds of "mild" customs were built during this period. As before, the cars were greatly lowered, stripped of all ornamentation and clad with fender skirts. For those with the cash, the sky was the limit, for in the skilled hands of Sam Barris, of Barris Kustom City, and a few other craftsmen, the top could be chopped and flowed into the body lines, the wings lengthened and blended in, and so on. The prolific Barris's are popularly credited with the first chopped post-war Mercury, built around 1950. The 1949 and later cars from Ford's Mercury division were an instant hit with their long, smooth, rounded shape, ideal for customising. The equivalent Ford model was boxier and less well received but eventually, this too found a place in the hearts of customisers. The Barris shop was involved with many of the chopped Fords and Mercuries of the period, typically relieving the roof of around four inches.

It's perhaps appropriate to point out that

todays rapport between rodders and customisers did not exist during this formative period. In fact, there was often a great deal of animosity between the two camps. Customs, or "lead sleds", (a reference to the considerable amount of body lead used in the alterations) were built for looks and style, whereas rods were built for racing on the dirt tracks or lake beds. If an early coupe received a roof chop, it was merely to reduce its wind resistance and hence increase its speed, not enhance its looks. One group preferred style, the other performance, never the twain meeting!

Despite this mutual distrust, the custom trend continued to increase in popularity. Cars began to appear right across America, no longer limited to California.

The very "isolation" of these new customisers led to certain shifts in emphasis as their cars were built. Perhaps because of the considerable body modifications involved, many of these later models tended to become "accessorised" rather

than aerodynamically cleaned-up. This may have been due to the lack of facilities and necessary experience outside the immediate West Coast area. It may also have been that the mutual "rubbing of shoulders" and swapping of ideas with like-minded people was denied to them. Whatever the reasons, the newer cars tended to be much less radically modified. Generally they were lowered and various additions bolted on. The results, when combined with complex, "over-the-top" paint schemes, often made the cars look very cluttered and considerably less visually appealing than their unmodified counterparts. This was a trend that was to be repeated, at various times in Britain, as the first fumbling attempts at customising began.

The first tangible trans-Atlantic influences began to appear in Britain, albeit on a very small scale, sometime around the mid to late 50s. The Mk I Consul, Zephyr and Zodiac were some of the first recipients of American styling ideas although, at the

The post-war Mercuries were "number one" favourites with customisers. This 1950s example with its sleek, long, low lines made it a natural choice. Countless Mercuries of this period were customised in America, a large number being lowered and chopped. Many, such as this example, retained much of the original running gear.

This Mk I Consul has received the full custom treatment and has been de-badged, de-handled, and had the front and rear aprons blended in. The suspension has been drastically lowered and quad headlights added. Moon discs and a single colour paint scheme complete the look.

time, their American cousins were coming into their period of excess chrome and tail-fins. Despite the dissimilarities, British cars began to appear with white-wall tyres, two-tone paint, external sun visors and the odd "continental kit". The latter consisted of a vertically mounted spare wheel assembly fitted at the rear extremity of the car. Virtually all modifications of the period were of the home-grown variety, the industry supplying the American custom scene not existing elsewhere, especially in post-war Britain where motoring was still the prerogative of relatively few people.

The arrival of the Mk II Consul, Zephyr and Zodiac saw an increase in the American influence. These looked more like American cars, with full-width grilles and a fair amount of chromework in the form of bumpers, over-riders, side-trim and even tail-fins. Typically, the cars were "accessorised" rather than customised, body modifications being uncommon. White-walls, two-tones, extra lights and ornamentation, port-holes and aerials became the order of the day. The infamous leopard-skin upholstery also arrived around this period!

Continental kits were still popular and graced many a Mk II's rear-end. A certain amount of tuning and performance equipment started to appear, a spin-off from saloon car circuit-racing, however, the majority of modifications were still in the form of "bolt-ons". There were no custom wheels available, so standard wheels were embellished with white-walls, hub-caps and spinners.

The British idea of bolting on as many accessories as possible was to continue for many years, with custom bodywork modifications being minimal. A number of good-looking cars *did* appear during this period, as did a large number of overdone monsters! The majority of these latter cars were in the hands of youngsters, so perhaps the lack of heavy body modification is not so surprising. To be done properly requires money and/or experience, both often lacking in this age group.

This "accessory" period was, to some extent, paralleled in America, as during the 50s, the interest in custom building had gradually spread to the four corners of the country. Perhaps for the same reasons as in Britain, many cars became the victims of the "accessory excess", with only minimal body modifications. In many people's eyes on both sides of the Atlantic, these became "custom cars". With the passage of time, most of these cars disappeared and in Britain in particular, it was not until well into the 60s that a few true customs began to appear.

The interest in both customs and "accessory customs" continued in America but

was suddenly curtailed in the early 60s, a victim of yet another automotive phenomenon to burst on the scene, the arrival of the "muscle car". For a long time, interest in customising waned and allegiance shifted to the drag-orientated, street-driven monsters and has only been rekindled in recent years. In America, old customs have been dragged from fields, barns and garages and lovingly brought back to life, often looking better than they originally did. There has been no real parallel to this in Britain, mainly because of customising's late start here.

True customs in Britain have always been

Notice the continental kit gracing the rear of this early Capri. This is a particularly well made example, many were much cruder. The Capri was one of the sleekest, and most stylish of Ford's offerings of the period. It has managed to retain its popularity throughout the past two decades and still has a strong following today. The chrome wire wheels with white-walls and white interior give the car a very definite American look.

An example of a mildly customised Mk II Consul. The car features chromed wire wheels, two-tone paintwork, tunnelled aerials and a continental kit at the rear. Although the style is reminiscent of the 1950s era, the overall quality of today's cars is much higher. Most Mark IIs are generally of all-steel construction, few fibre-glass panels being available.

CUSTOM Fords

comparatively rare beasts for a number of reasons, perhaps the main one being a basic lack of suitable vehicles to apply predominantly American ideas to. This has resulted in British customs acquiring a flavour of their own, with Fords, as usual, figuring high on the popularity list. Mk I, II and, to a lesser extent, Mk III, Consul, Zephyr and Zodiacs have all been the recipients of the true custom treatment. Most other models have been similarly treated, but in lesser numbers. The 100E range, as a custom "base" has increased in

recent years, as has, perhaps surprisingly, the 105E Anglia. Most other models seem to wax and wane in terms of popularity.

Despite the appearance of British Ford-based customs, in many people's eyes the best customs are still those based on the traditional American Fords of the late 30s to mid 50s. These are, not surprisingly, very thin on the ground in Britain. Clearly, most of the techniques and styles were developed around the particular size and shape of the American models and these do not always transfer well to the traditionally

47

smaller British cars. The few customs based on American models of this era to be found in Britain, have almost invariably been imported rather than built here. Ford models from the late 30s and early 40s seem to be most popular, along with a few late 40s and early 50s Mercuries. Clearly the costs involved in importing one of these period classics can be enormous, however, they make a superb and very welcome addition to the custom scene in Britain.

As the 60s became the 70s, a number of other Ford products were adopted by the, mainly young, customisers. The Capri, with its sporty looks, had always been popular with the younger generation, the result being that over a decade, thousands were "customised". As a rule, this involved raising the rear of the car with a set of longer rear spring shackles (the infamous "jack-up" kit), big wheels at the back and often as many accessories as possible tacked on. In the public's eye, these were "custom cars", nothing in fact, being farther from the truth. Fortunately, this craze eventually petered out leaving the better built survivors.

The majority had attempted to emulate the drag racing look, in some cases very successfully. These cars became widely known as examples of "Street Machines" and were really the modern day equivalents of the earlier Hot/Street-Rods. Most of the modifications reflected the styles of the quarter mile although frequently they were only skin deep. Many may have looked as if they had just escaped from the drag strip, but underneath the cosmetic restyling, most of the mechanical parts were left untouched.

In later years, engine transplants became more common. Especially popular was Ford's 3 litre V6, followed closely by the Rover V8 and Chevrolet small-block. Many Capris were treated to a set of body extras, usually taking the form of a front air dam, bonnet bulge or scoop, boot spoiler and in some cases, side skirts. Regrettably in a lot of cases, the enthusiasm exceeded the bodyworking capabilities of the owner!

The late 70s saw the appearance of a number of much more tastefully styled Capris, with well blended additional panels, lowered suspension, X-pack arches and subtle, single colour paint schemes. These were perhaps, the forerunners of the styles that came to be almost universally adopted during the 1980s as the "body styling kit" became widely available.

During this period, the other main favourite of the "juvenile customiser" was the ubiquitous Cortina in its many forms.

This 1938 Fordson van was originally built by Robyn Slater and later updated by Alistair Papworth. It features a home-built box-section chassis that houses a 2.5 litre Daimler V8 and BW 35 autobox. The motor is fed from a Mazda four-barrel carburettor. The front suspension is Vauxhall Viva fitted with Victor discs and Spax shock absorbers. The rear suspension is an S-type Jaguar IRS, narrowed seven inches each side and fitted with Triumph Herald coil-overs. The body was chopped three inches, fitted with steel Prefect arches, a two slot grill and punched full of louvres. These little commercials have always been popular with rodders although there are relatively few survivors.

This step-side pick-up conversion was based on a conventional Saloon, and was built by aircraft engineer, Steve Woodley. The chassis was lengthened by fourteen inches and the front half of the body turned into the cab. All of the compound curves involved in the metalwork were made by the owner. He was also responsible for moulding the rear fibre-glass arches and building the aluminium/wood bed. The Ford V6 that provides the power, features many hand-made aluminium and stainless steel components. Likewise, the Jaguar IRS also has many unique touches. The end result is very stylish. What a pity Ford never made one!

Built by Nick Lang, this black 1954 Popular features a home-built box section chassis, now housing a 3-litre Ford V6 with a C4 autobox. The rear suspension is from an S-type Jaguar and the front, from a Triumph Vitesse. The use of steel wheels fitted with Moon discs gives the car a 1950s look, although the fibre-glass panels, low stance and sophisticated interior mean that it could only be a much later car.

Yet another example of the ubiquitous Popular, this time with a difference. The two-seater convertible conversion had been superbly carried out by Russ White using a boxed chassis and a 1957 body. As an additional styling exercise, the boot lid had been punched full of louvres. The front suspension is an HA Viva unit with Kawasaki 1000 motorcycle springs and the rear, an S-type Jaguar IRS. The engine is now a 3 litre V6 and autobox from a

INSET: A fine pair of rodded Populars. The nearer of the two has been chopped and powered by a Rover V8 and autobox. It features a reproduction three-slot grill and a steel roof insert. The other car has black glass, fibre-glass wings and Ford V6 power.

This Mk II Zodiac, built by
Kevin Rooney, has been given
a long, sleek, custom look.
Subtle lowering, slightly flared
rear arches, continental kit and
white upholstery gives a 1950s
theme. Power originally came
from a Daimler V8 although
this was later switched to a
Rover unit. The car was badly
damaged when a propshaft
joint disintegrated, smashing
the floor, gearbox and radiator.
Clearly, it was soon rebuilt to
its former high standard.

INSET: A former drag car returned to the street. This 100E Popular was constructed from a part-built drag car and was originally intended to run in the "Street" classes, using a turbocharged 1500 Ford engine. It was rebuilt using Mk II Escort front suspension 1500 GT engine, Anglia gearbox and Cortina rear axle mounted on 100E springs. The car also featured a tilt-front, Peugeot grill and Triumph 1300 steering column. Note the wide alloy wheels have been kept under the standard width arches.

This 105E Anglia features many subtle additions. A Capri "power bulge" has been added to the bonnet and the lower aprons carefully blended in. The wheel arches have been neatly flared and an additional set of rear lights grafted on. The power is provided by a 1500 GT Ford engine. The car abounds with clever ideas and well executed touches.

A neat pick-up conversion based on a Mk I Cortina. Alloy wheels and tasteful graphics complete the look. This conversion has resulted in a surprisingly stylish pick-up, an option never offered by Ford.

INSET: **A clever pick-up conversion constructed by K. Portsmouth. The off-road style hauler was based on a 1970 Mk II Cortina. The much-modified body now sits on a home-built box-section chassis which is also home for the Ford V6 that now provides the power. The front axle is a narrowed Transit unit, mounted on leaf springs. With its large wheels and tyres and high stance, it manages to look remarkably like one of the current crop of Japanese mini-trucks.**

A modern example of "professional customising". This conversion has involved the removal of the Capri's roof. A complex, but completely inconspicuous, system of bracing has put back the lost strength, the result being less body flexing than before the conversion. The car also sports extended and modified RS arches and sill extensions. The wheels are now 7x15 RS items. A very stylish conversion, aptly named the "Capriolet". Mechanically the car is unaltered, a standard 2.8i Capri engine hiding under the bonnet.

INSET: A stylish custom look has been given to this Mk I Escort van that was based on a battered builders van. A fully detailed four-cylinder engine supplies the power, a host of new panels and parts replacing the well-worn originals. With the owner being an electronics expert, all of the electrics plus many extras are contained in a custom compartment in the rear floor. The body was treated to subtle graphic paintwork and included tunnelled aerials and extra windows. Virtually all of the innovative additions were home built.

The Super Van II. This Transit has been described as the "fastest delivery van in the world". The carbon fibre reinforced body houses independent front and rear suspensions, five-speed Hewland gearbox and a mid-mounted 3.9-litre Cosworth V8. This produces around 590 bhp giving a 0-60 time of three seconds (0-100 in 6.5 seconds) and a top speed of over 180 mph! The van was built by Auto Racing Technology for Ford's European Truck Operation at a reputed cost of £100,000. With its racing body kit attached it has lapped Silverstone at an average speed of 108.7 mph. This vehicle supersedes Super Van I, built in the 70s and powered by a 435 hp Gurney-Weslake engine giving 137 mph top speed (courtesy Ford Motor Company).

CUSTOM Fords

These were often used as base vehicles, often because they were cheap enough to be a youngster's first car. These tended to receive similar treatment to the Capris, with jacked-up rear, big rear wheels, side pipes and an assortment of tack-on panels and accessories. As before, these largely faded away as the 70s drew to a close, to be replaced by much more tastefully re-worked cars. Although less common, in terms of sheer numbers, these later Cortinas, as with the Capris, generally had better bodywork, lowered suspension and were built to a much higher standard than their predecessors. These too began to reflect a change away from the styling of the drag strip towards the smoother, lower cars of the racing circuits.

Ford's smaller and ever-popular Escort range, rather surprisingly, never seems to have been widely used as a custom base. Those that were customised usually emulated the drag strip styles of their larger brethren. Perhaps because of their smaller size, they appear to have responded less successfully than the larger

Capris and Cortinas. Some of the most striking Escorts of the period were based around the RS 2000 range. When lowered, fitted with X-pack arches, wider wheels and a good paint job, these diminutive road-burners looked superb and were capable of out-performing cars that cost ten times their price. Generally speaking, the various Escort models were not widely used as customs, the majority of modified versions being styled on the innumerable rally cars that were being raced so successfully at the time.

The newer British Fords have been rather less frequently customised, partially as their "new", aerodynamic shape does not respond particularly well to the

An example of the many body styling kits that became available for Ford models during the 1980s. This Capri has been transformed by the addition of spoilers, skirts, grille infill and wheels. The circuit racing influence is quite apparent (courtesy Kat).

traditional techniques and styles, but mainly because other influences have been at work. The advent of the "body styling kit" has meant a shift has once again occurred, in terms of popularity, the current look owing much to the influence of circuit racing. The situation is somewhat akin to that in America when muscle cars appeared, sweeping everything else aside. Interest in other forms of automotive

Body styling of the 1980s. This XR3i has been modified by the addition of spoiler, valance and sill extensions and stylish rear light louvres. The style of the completed car shows some similarities to Ford's recent ill-fated RS 1700 (courtesy XL Designs).

expression were only to reappear some years later. Perhaps the same situation is destined to happen here. In a decade, we may well see chopped, fender-skirted, ground-hugging Sierras, Escorts and Granadas cruising the streets! Until then, it seems that the older Fords will continue to form the basis of the majority of custom projects.

Roaring roadsters to Street-Rods

Throughout the custom world's various ups and downs, the performance-related side of things continued to expand. The immediate post-war period in America saw a further burst of activity on the roadster/hot-rod front, this time largely centred on the oval dirt-tracks. Once again, California spawned another form of racing specifically for the stripped-down T, A and B roadsters. Some of the lakes racers changed their allegiance and began to vie with each other directly, rather than against the clock. The cars were basically the same, mainly a combination of high and low-boy early roadsters, running an assortment of Ford engines. This form of track racing eventually became known as the "Roaring Roadsters".

The roadsters were modified to suit the oval-tracks, more emphasis now being put on suspension arrangements. Gear ratios were lowered as top speed was no longer the main requirement. Unlike the lakes, aerodynamics played little part, hence streamlining was unnecessary. These stripped-down, hotted-up roadsters were almost totally devoid of safety equipment but despite this, there appear to have been comparatively few casualties. They formed the basis of a cheap way to go racing.

Its popularity grew, as this form of motor sport was not isolated high across the mountains, but easily accessible from the major centres of population. As with the lakes, few participants trailered their cars to race meetings, many doubling as daily transport for the owners.

Apart from the lakes and the oval-tracks, the only other avenue for the would-be racer was on the streets, this illegal and potentially dangerous practice still being carried on in increasing numbers.

The late 40s and early 50s saw an explosion in the interest in hot-rodding in general, with its popularity spreading far beyond the boundaries of its birth place, California. Much of this spread can be attributed to the many young ex-servicemen, some of whom were also involved in boosting the interest in customising, returning after the war and now in search of excitement.

The initial emphasis was, as with California, centred around Ford roadsters, however, many soon discovered that Californian styles were not necessarily suited to the more inhospitable climates of other regions. Whereas a lack of top, windshield and wings was fine for California, it was not so good if rain or snow

had to be dealt with on a regular basis. California had its sunshine, lake beds and oval-tracks to race on, the majority of the others had the rain and the streets. A gradual change in requirements and emphasis became apparent as hot-rods began to appear with tops, wings, upholstery and even the occasional heater!

Where there was no access to racing activity, performance began to take second place behind practicality and comfort. Paintwork, trim and overall quality of workmanship became more important. "Hot-rodding" gradually became "Street-rodding", a concession to the increasing needs of many for a car that could be used all year round, in all kinds of weathers. About 95% of all hot/street rods of the period were Fords, the majority being Model T, A, B and 40 with a lesser number of late 30s cars. The unwritten rule was "If it isn't a Ford, then it isn't a rod!"

The early 50s saw the first appearance of the fabled Ardun OHV conversion heads for the side-valve V8. Designed by Zora Arkus-Duntov, they featured hemispherical combustion chambers and an outboard cooling system. These aftermarket bolt-on heads immediately found a place in the hearts and engine bays of performance buffs and are still highly prized items, even today.

Although Britain had no hot-rodding activity at the time, perhaps one of the nearest examples to it was being produced between 1950 and 1953 by Allards. They built a number of cars powered by Ford's V8, fitted with the power-boosting Ardun heads. Many Allards were exported, less engine, to America, where they were fitted with either a Chrysler or Cadillac V8, the British versions mainly using the Ford-Ardun. Sidney Allard, the car's creator, drove a Ford-powered version in the 1950 Le Mans race, finishing a creditable third in his "Four wheeled motorcycle". True hot/street rods were not destined to appear in Britain for some years.

In the mid 50s, something happened in America that boosted the interest and popularity of the ubiquitous Model T, almost overnight. The phenomenom was the advent of the TV series "77 Sunset Strip", in which one of the central characters, "Kookie" Burns, drove a Cadillac-powered 1923 T Roadster. The car caught the imagination of youngsters across America and before long, thousands of clone cars and various other versions were on the streets. Naturally, as ideas gradually spread across from the US, a few rodded Ts began to find their way onto British roads. In the early 60s, Model T bodies and chassis became the first street-rod "kit" to become generally available to the public. The result was many weird and wonderful creations before people finally got it right in terms of style and proportion.

Meanwhile, the American muscle car phenomenom of the 60s threatened to sweep away interest from many other forms of automotive expression. Customs all but disappeared and interest in street-rodding diminished substantially. It was only after many years that the latter began to make a comeback, now constituting a major hobby/sport in America. The number and quality of street-rods has risen steadily over the years, to a point where major car shows now attract thousands of entries, the majority of them still Ford-based.

For many years the Model T remained top of the American street-rod list and still managed to remain in favour even during the muscle car period.

In Britain, there was virtually no true street-rodding until the late 50s and then only on a small scale. There were no magazines, no specialist suppliers, no manufacturers, only a few individuals with an interest in what was happening on the American scene. Unlike America, there were no fibre-glass bodies available, consequently, what few rods there were, were invariably based on original steel

The rear end of this Model T consists of a fully chromed, de-caged Jaguar IRS. This was the hot set-up for the 1970s and although they looked superb, they were both heavy and expensive to maintain and repair. Many first-time rodders came to grief using these, as installation was much more critical and complex compared with a conventional live axle. The 1980s saw the Jaguar IRS begin to lose favour.

Murals and cartoons were a form of automotive art that was popular during the 1960s and early 1970s. More recent cars have remained relatively unadorned. Single colour paint schemes have become the order of the day with both solid colours and metallic finishes being used. Perhaps the one exception to this is with large vans where murals are often used to break up the large expanses of sheet metal.

models. There were a handful of British built Model As and Bs as well as a smattering of 103E Populars. Modifications in most cases were totally home-brewed.

Things began to really take off in the early 60s with the first fibre-glass Model T bodies becoming available. Britain began to see a few open-engined Ts on its roads, the majority of them using parts from small domestic cars. Four-cylinder Ford engines, gearboxes and rear axles were widely used items. Many of these early Ts suffered badly in terms of proportions and incompatibility of the various visual aspects, however by the late 60s, American styles had been adapted and modified to suit the British requirements and Ts generally looked much better. One major difference between British and American Ts was that the latter often ran without wings although their British cousins were legally obliged to cover (at least partially) all four wheels. Not surprisingly, this led to a higher incidence of full-bodied Model Ts in Britain.

As the 60s drew to a close, a greater variety of fibre-glass bodies and chassis started to become available. Car clubs

were formed and magazines began to take interest in what was now attracting a much wider assortment of people.

As usual, the majority of rods of the period were of Ford origin, most of them still retaining steel bodies and often, much of the original running gear. From now until the early 70s, a much greater spread of vehicle types were used as the basis for street-rods. Ford Model As, Bs, Ys, Pilots and "sit-up-and-beg" Populars (Pops) were all successfully used. Whereas the Consul, Zephyr, Zodiac range tended to be used as custom building material, the others responded more favourably to the traditional hot-rod styles. In later years, as interest in drag racing escalated, these too started to appear on the streets, looking as if they had just escaped from the nearest drag strip.

Engine transplanting became much more widespread during this period, the four-cylinder OHV and later OHC Ford engines powering large numbers of street-rods. Ford, Chevrolet and Rover V8s became popular as power-plants for larger cars such as As, Bs and Pilots, whereas the four-cylinders tended to find homes in countless Ts, Ys, 100Es and 103E Populars. The latter assumed a major role and became the backbone of British street-rodding, in a similar manner to the role that the Model B/18 had assumed in America. Innumerable reproduction parts became available for the "Pop", including glass wings, sills and boot lids, as well as numerous small parts such as window rubbers and trim components. Complete replacement chassis also appeared from a number of sources.

The diminuitive Model Y was another favourite around this period, with glass-fibre bodies, panels and complete chassis also becoming available, although to a lesser degree than for the Pop.

The 103E Popular formed the basis of a large number of street-rod projects. Apart from the numerous saloon versions, the humble Popular was transformed into a fascinating assortment of vehicles. A number of coupe versions were built as well as several convertibles. Pick-ups and various van-type versions were also created from Ford's economy runabout.

Throughout the 1970s, both in America and Britain, different styles found favour at different times. The early part of the decade saw a great upsurge in interest in the "Resto-Rod". Basically, this involved a meticulous restoration of the car's bodywork plus retention of all the original trim and accessories, the mechanical parts being replaced by more modern components. It was during this period that the various small parts, such as cowl lights and grille badges, that had previously been discarded, began to assume such importance and hence increased dramatically in price. As a consequence, it was not long before the after-market industries began to reproduce innumerable replacement parts, especially for Fords.

The end result of this trend, especially in America, was that a great number of rods began to look very similar to each other, thus rather defeating the ideal of building an "individual" car. Probably as a consequence of this, there was a swing away from the resto styles, back towards the "hot-rod" look of the 1950s and early

An example of a Popular rodded in the early 1970s. Notice both rodding and customising ideas that tended to overlap during this period. The padded roof, panelled windows and eight spoke wheels were less frequently seen in later years. The power was provided by an Austin-Healey Sprite engine and gearbox. The front suspension was based around the HA Viva, a set-up that was destined to become commonly used as a result of its low cost and ease of fitting. As with many cars of the time, no fibre-glass panels were used. The chassis was a strengthened original and the rear axle from an Anglia van.

1960s. As this new breed of rod emerged, it became clear that although the styling reflected this earlier period, the engineering greatly surpassed that of most of their predecessors. Roadsters in particular, were built smooth and fenderless, as were the early lakes racers, however that's where the similarity ended.

Underneath the simple looking bodies often lurked a "high-tech" chassis with full independent front and rear suspensions, disc brakes on all four wheels and a supercharged V8 engine. Further refinement was to follow in the form of engine and chassis components made of stainless steel or milled and machined from solid billets of aluminium. A race seemed to be on to see who could produce the most exotic (and expensive) rod parts. The end result was a small elite whose cars were so advanced and exotic that the techniques they embodied were completely beyond the reach of the average street-rodder. The high-tech, "state of the art" street-rod had arrived. Although much of this happened in America, it was paralleled, to a lesser extent on the British scene.

Possibly as a reaction to these unaffordable cars, there was renewed interest in the more basic and easily built

CUSTOM fords

rods. Independent suspensions lost some ground to solid rear axles and "buggy-sprung" fronts. The universally accepted V8 began to face competition from some of the newer and smaller V6 and high performance four-cylinder engines that had been appearing in recent years. Generally, cars got simpler to build and maintain but still retained a high degree of engineering excellence.

Around this time, a section of the rodding fraternity suddenly realised that a whole part of their heritage was slipping away,

The back view of this Popular shows the trend towards the clean lines of recent years. Note the lack of hinges and handles and the cleverly flared-in rear lights. Unlike its earlier counterparts, glass-fibre panels have been extensively used, good steel panels becoming increasingly difficult to locate. The car, built by Mervin King, is powered by a Rover V8 and the independent front and rear suspension come, unusually, from a Lotus Elan.

almost unnoticed. The early street and lakes racers, the cars that formed the real roots of rodding, had all but disappeared. With this in mind, they set about attempting to re-create these early cars before they became completely lost in the mists of time. Abandoned chassis were salvaged, old tuning equipment refurbished and Ford side-valve V8s lovingly rebuilt. Before long, rods began to appear looking as if they had stepped from the pages of the history books. These became known as "Nostalgia-Rods" and although not common, particularly in Britain, helped to remind the younger rodders of today, where their interest had originated from.

Where are we today? Both in America and Britain, the street rodding scene now consists of a mixture of styles from a number of different eras. It's not uncommon to see nostalgia, resto and high-tech cars all mingled together at rodding events. The previous trend of adopting new styles to the exclusion of all others, seems to have disappeared. The result has been a marvellous mixture of sights, sounds and colours from over a span of five decades or more.

What does the future hold? Probably the diversity will increase as rodders adopt ideas and influences from other spheres of automotive activity. A few cars are beginning to appear that owe much of their styling and appearance more to the European circuit racers than to the drag strips or the lakes. Possibly this trend will develop and predominate for a few years, but it seems probable that, because of its very individualistic nature, rodders will continue to put together a wide assortment of, predominantly, Ford-based rods for many years to come!

The immaculate engine bay of this Mk II Zephyr reveals a fully detailed, blown Rover V8. The clever use of chrome plating, polished aluminium and anodising makes this power plant a knockout. The old four and six-cylinder engines are rarely retained as they were both heavy and, by today's standards, low powered. The Rover V8 has found a place in many Rods as apart from being fairly powerful, its lightweight all-aluminium construction often minimises suspension uprating problems.

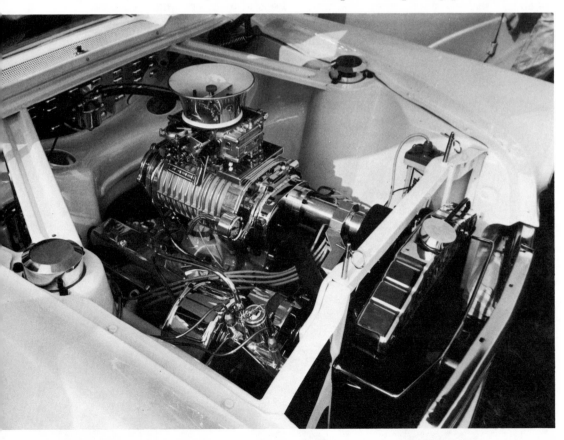

The quarter mile dash!

The period around 1950 saw furious activity on the American automotive front, with an upsurge in interest and activity in a number of forms of racing and rodding. In California, and to a lesser extent elsewhere, the police and civil authorities were still having severe problems as a result of the prolific street-racing that was being carried on. Whereas California had its lakes and ovals to relieve the pressure, other areas lacked any form of organised racing or rodding activity. What many areas *did* gave was plenty of old, abandoned airfields and it was these that eventually gave a home to yet another form of racing, one that was to have a significant effect on the style of street cars for decades to follow. Drag racing had arrived!

Drag racing started in earnest´ in June 1950, with the opening of a strip on a disused runway at Santa Ana airfield in California. Initially there were no classes, V8-powered roadsters racing alongside four-cylinder cars. Flag starts were used and timing carried out simply with a stop watch. Numerous strips soon sprang up and before long it became clear that some form of organising body was needed, this coming into being in 1951 with the formation of the National Hot Rod Association. By the mid 50s, classing arrangements had been sorted out and the first purpose-built drag cars began to replace many of the Ford-based street/strip cars that regularly pounded down the quarter mile. The tried-and-tested Ford V8 saw service in many of the cars, including many of the early dragsters that appeared. It was to be a long time before the venerable flat-head V8 was to be completely ousted by the newer OHV Cadillac, Buick and Chevrolet V8s and later by the famed Chrysler hemi.

Drag racing went from strength to strength. Because of the easy access, more of the lakes racers defected, now preferring to race side by side on the drag strips. Public interest also increased as people from the cities became aware of this exciting new sport sprouting, quite literally, on their doorsteps. The period

CUSTOM Fords

between 1955 and 1960 reflected this enthusiasm, with tremendous advances being made, as cars were built and set up, with the quarter mile dash in mind.

Not surprisingly, drag racing had a tremendous influence on street-driven cars. The big rear/skinny front wheel combination quickly became adopted and later, the nose-down stance. The styles and trends set by the drag cars were perhaps, the single most influential factor to be applied to street cars. Before long, not only were "traditional" rods given the treatment, newer show-room models also began to appear with the nose-down, balloon rear tyre look. The magazines of the period were full of Fords, from lakes racing Ts to drag-styled late models. At the time, Ford were the undisputed favourite in what was known as the "youth market" and it did not take them long to begin to capitalise on it.

Late 1962 saw the emergence of a new breed of hot-rod, with the introduction of the "Factory Experimental" (FX) cars. These were thinly disguised full-blown drag racers, built with the main aim of outperforming all competition on the strip and at the same time impressing potential buyers. The first offerings from Ford came in the shape of a number of stripped and lightened Galaxies. These were superseded in 1963 by the "Ford Thunderbolts", which were based on the ever-popular Fairlane. These cars were nothing short of factory-built hot-rods. Ford took fifty Fairlanes off the production line, gutted them and fitted 427 ci V8s (giving around 500 bhp) and either 4 or 5-speed gearboxes. These would run the quarter mile in around 11 seconds with terminal speeds in the region of 125 mph, very respectable figures for the times.

In 1964, with the co-operation of the

Lincoln-Mercury division, the legendary American drag-racer Jack Chrisman, squeezed a 427 ci Ford motor into a basically standard Comet. It was raced throughout America and, not surprisingly, attracted a great deal of public interest. A year later, with the aid of Bill Stroppe and Gene Mooneyham, Chrisman took one of the new Ford Single Overhead Cam (SOHC) engines and fitted it into a dramatically lightened, rebuilt version of the 1964 car. The car now sported a fibre-glass front-end and a well set back supercharged, injected engine running on nitromethane/methanol fuel. There was no gearbox, merely a direct drive to the 9" Ford back axle. The car caused a sensation and was soon running the quarter mile in around 9.5 seconds at speeds in excess of 160 mph. 1966 saw the appearance of a pair of all glass-bodied, tubular-chassis Comets, from which the lineage of the current crop of ultra-sophisticated "Funny Cars" can easily be traced.

As with many other forms of motor sport, both before and after the appearance of drag racing, a long-running battle took place between Ford and its two main rivals, General Motors and Chrysler, as all three fought it out for the "Super Stock" and "A/Factory Experimental" classes.

By early 1965, the newly introduced Mustang was playing its part at the drags. With heavy Ford Motor Company backing and sponsorship, the ultra-light, glass-bodied, nitro-burning, injected, 427 ci fastback Mustangs evolved and soon dominated their classes. 1966 onwards saw Ford's SOHC "pony cars" completely dominate the inappropriately named "Stock" classes. Five successful seasons followed before Ford, in 1970, abruptly pulled out of its drag racing programme. Following this, the few teams who continued running Ford SOHC and Boss 429 motors soon found the spares situation getting progressively worse. Before long, they too, ceased to use these venerable motors.

The next two decades saw drag racing expand in America to form the multi-million dollar industry that it has now become. Ford Motor Company have been involved

An example of a "Competition Altered" drag car built and raced by Graham Peake. It features a heavily modified Model T body and is powered by a hot RS 2000 motor. The transmission is via a clutch operated BW 35 autobox, modified for manual operation. The rear axle is a much-narrowed Austin Westminster unit. Typical quarter mile times are in the region of 11.5 seconds with terminal speeds of 120 mph.

at various times and in various ways but has never repeated its factory-backed drag-racing activities of the 1960s. Today, countless Ford models still run in a number of classes although the resemblance to showroom cars is often only skin deep.

In recent years, Ford have shown renewed interest, largely as a result of its multifaceted "Racing into the future" programme. The blue Ford logo is currently to be seen on a number of different cars, competing in a variety of motor sports. Among the best known in drag racing circles, is probably the "Pro-stock" Thunderbird of Rickie Smith and the "Funny Car" of Kenny Bernstein.

In the lower classes there has always been a high proportion of Ford-based cars. The spin-off from these creations of the

quarter mile is to be seen daily reflected on the streets, where a multitude of cosmetically-similar cars are to be found. Many of today's drag cars are too specialised and over-powered to be practical for highway use but their influence on the styling of their humbler street-driven brethren can be seen across America.

Drag racing in Britain has been a different story. Apart from a few individuals, there was no drag racing activity in Britain until well into the early 1960s. The nearest thing were a number of "sprints", some of which dated back to the 1920s. The major difference was that at these events, racing was against the clock and not directly against another competitor. It was not until 1964, when organised drag racing had been in existence for over a decade, that Britain got its first real taste of action. In that year, two of America's top drag racers, "TV" Tommy Ivo and Don Garlits, brought their dragsters over in order to put on a number of exhibition runs. There were no drag strips, the runs being made at such places as Blackbush airfield. Crowds of over 20,000 turned out to see the two Americans and a handful of British competitors in action. The following two years saw further visits by American teams and an upsurge in interest in Britain. Gradually, British cars began to appear and by the end of 1966, Santa Pod Raceway, Britain's first permanent drag strip, existed. As in America, the looks of the strip began to be reflected on the streets as the British too, began to apply the styles to their domestic cars.

As time passed, organising bodies were formed, regulations agreed upon and classing arrangements sorted out. Inevitably, the lower classes had plenty of Fords running in them, from hotted-up Model T street rods, to showroom models, many being driven to great success. The more competitive and expensive classes,

as with America, began to become so specialised as to restrict their use to strip-driven cars only.

Some of the most popular cars to emerge during this period were what came to be known as the "Competition Altereds". These were generally full-blown dragsters that were required to retain some semblance of a recognisable body. The skimpy Model T body was especially popular, although often cut and altered in a variety of ways. The retention of a "recognisable" body meant that spectators could still identify, to a certain extent, with their own road-going vehicles. As a consequence, these short wheel based, over-powered "street-rods" remained the crowd's favourite over a long period. Not surprisingly, people began to build street-driven Model Ts that resembled the Altereds, a style, although lacking practicality, that still remains popular today.

In Britain, the Model T has been joined by virtually every other Ford ever made, as over the years, the drag strip's looks and styling have been adapted to street-driven cars in large numbers. Early "traditional" rods have received the treatment, as well as pre-war "upright" Fords and post-war slab-sided models. These have been joined by innumerable 60s and 70s cars such as Capris and Cortinas. The trend continues, as one of the current top British "genuine" drag cars is the full-bodied Sierra of Sylvia Hauser. We shall probably see similar looking road-going versions appearing in the next few years.

It appears that as long as drag racing exists, the ever-popular blue logo will continue to be seen. The result of this, whether as a result of individuals or of Ford itself, will undoubtedly mean plenty of strip-styled Fords of all eras prowling the streets, certainly well into the forseeable future.

CHAPTER THREE

Model Ts and Model As

This era saw the emergence of the cars that really started off the whole rodding scene. The Model Ts were the first to be rodded in both their original form and later, as the first widely available "kit-rods".

One of the initial reasons for their popularity was their cheapness, a factor no longer true today. The surviving original Ts are now worth a lot of money and consequently, are nowadays rarely used by rodders. Apart from the potential cost and lack of availability, with the exception of the body and a few ancillaries, there is very little of the T that would be of use to a modern day rodder. Virtually all of today's Ts are based around reproduction chassis (some home-built and others commercially available) with glass-fibre bodies. The latter have been available for over two decades in Britain and can form the basis of an economical way to go rodding. They can also form the basis of a very expensive route as many of today's most sophisticated and visually awesome engines are to be found nestling between the chassis rails of a Model T.

The majority of Ts have been based on a roadster body or variant, such as a roadster/pick-up. Full-bodied versions are much more uncommon in Britain, largely due to the lack of availability, either as a steel body or even in the form of a reproduction.

Left: **This traditional style Model T features a drop-tube front axle mounted on a transverse spring. Power is provided by a 2.5 litre Daimler V8. The little car is based on a reproduction chassis fitted with a Jaguar IRS and a fibre-glass body. Many hand-made brass and stainless parts are in evidence. The T was the first reproduction body to become widely available in both America and Britain. The "wings", a legal necessity in Britain, help distinguish this from its American counterpart which would almost certainly be lacking them.**

Facing page, Top: This 1927 Model T "Doctor's Coupe" is almost certainly unique in Britain. It was originally built in the States with Chevrolet power, but now runs with a Ford 2 litre OHC engine. The sophisticated drive-train and chassis feature many one-off components constructed by one of Britain's top rod builders, Nick Butler. The all-steel resto-styled body has been beautifully restored and painted Henry's favourite colour, black! Any minor bodywork blemishes soon become apparent when a dark paint finish is used, clearly there are none here, the sheet metal being perfect.

Right: This low-slung Model T is powered by the ubiquitous Rover V8. The front end consists of a tube-axled "suicide" system with motorcycle wheels. Despite the uncertain British weather and that this style lacks practicality, it still remains popular. The power to weight ratio of lightweight cars, such as this, with V8 power, often leads to impressive performance figures!

Above: Loosely modelled on a Model T C-cab, this truck is now powered by a Ford V6. The largely hand-built vehicle features a multitude of stainless steel and milled aluminium parts. The rear suspension is a modified independent unit from a Mk IV Zodiac, a set-up not commonly encountered. As with the majority of today's T-based rods, no original T parts were used. This unique truck has been aptly named "Fanta-C".

left: **This amazing Model T is powered by a supercharged Dick Landy-built 426 ci Chrysler hemi! The car is another of Nick Butler's efforts and features an incredibly complex suspension system, much of it hand made. This car uses a fibre-glass body and wings and is named "Andromeda". This is an example of what is termed "state-of-the-art".**

The other important car of this era is the Model A. Not so long ago, this was the poor cousin of the rodder's perennial favourite, the Model B/18. In recent years, as the cost of the B has escalated by such alarming proportions, rodders, especially in America, have turned their attention to the not dissimilar model A range. Many As have now been rodded, often retaining the steel bodies, some of which have survived in remarkably good condition. Roadsters, two-door sedans and later, four-door sedans have all appeared in increasing numbers in recent years. As a consequence, a large range of reproduction parts has become available. This includes complete chassis, hoods, replacement wood framing kits and a range of fibre-glass bodies. This is not to imply that the typical Model A street rod, with either a steel or glass body, is a cheap car! The cost, going via either route, is still often considerable, even in America where availability and price is still greatly in its favour.

Britain is in a different position as As have been fairly scarce for many years. Old cars tended to be recycled more quickly in Britain, many disappearing during the scrap-metal collections of World War II. As a result, the few genuine Model As that did survive are now worth considerable amounts of money. This obviously limits their use by the average rodder.

The only other option open is the fibre-glass repro body. These have been available for some years but, with a few exceptions, most British versions have required a great deal of re-working and fabrication in order to make them look even remotely authentic. American repros seem to have been of a much higher quality, but clearly the costs and difficulties of importing one can be enormous. This lack of availability has clearly restricted the number of Model A based-rods on British roads although the ones that do exist are generally of a very high standard.

Below:
This Model A three-window Coupe would look at home at an American rod run. The ever-popular drag style car features Chevrolet V8 power and dropped I-beam front axle. I-beam axles have lost some ground in recent years to tubular items and latterly to independent front suspensions. The traditional I-beam is still favoured by some die-hards. With the exception of the widened rear wings and top chop, the body is all stock.

This Model A Sedan shows today's trend towards clean lines. It lacks bonnet louvres and bumpers and features widened wings and a chopped top. The single colour paint scheme helps enhance its looks.

Below:
This immaculate Model A Roadster shows a number of current styling touches such as hidden hinges, no louvres or handles, aluminium windshield posts and stamped competition wheels. The Model A Roadster has become increasingly popular in recent years following the appearance of good quality fibre-glass bodies and reproduction chassis. Perhaps the most notable are Paul Haig's, whose company specialises in Model A-related parts.

Top:

This resto-styled rod is based on a Model A Cabriolet. Apart from the lack of bumpers and addition of alloy 5-spoke wheels, the car could pass for an excellent restoration. Underneath is a different story, with modern running gear.

Centre:

A unique example of a Briggs-bodied Model A Sedan built by John Cross. The Briggs body is unusual in that it lacks the rear side windows and is four inches wider than the standard body. A Haig chassis was used, this having an independent front and rear suspension. The extensive restoration of the body included a roof chop and louvre-less bonnet sides, as well as complete replacement of the wooden framing. Power is provided by a Rover V8 with autobox. The low stance, single colour paint scheme, Connolly hide interior and chrome wire wheels complete the look.

Bottom:

An example of a chopped reproduction Model A Sedan Delivery recently brought onto the British market. The styling reflects the contemporary high-tech, one-piece look currently finding favour in both Britain and America. This type of "kit rod" makes a good starting point and can be fitted with a variety of drive-trains. This particular example is powered by a four-cylinder Ford engine. Notice the use of rectangular headlights, horizontal grille slats and low stance, giving the car a distinctive look.

CUSTOM Fords

The Mk II Cortina Savage, a legend in its own time. The car shown was treated to a thorough rebuild, over a number of years, by the owner, Mike Birch. It is a Mk II Series I, built by Savages in 1968 and it is one of the few surviving 3000 E four-door overdrive models. Ford's 3-litre Essex V6 provided the power for these rapid cars, top speed being a very respectable 120 mph.

An XR2 Fiesta in racing trim. The Fiesta was Ford's first front-wheel drive offering for the British market. This car is raced in the Ford Credit Championship. For this type of motor sport, the engine and gearbox must remain unaltered. This particular example won the 1986 Championship, in the hands of Barry Williams.

This vintage hot-rod was created from a multitude of old parts by Berni Chodosh, using a 1932 chassis with most of the running gear coming from an assortment of 1940 Fords. The engine is a 24-stud sidevalve of 1942 vintage, bored out to 239 ci and fitted with many vintage tuning parts. This includes Offenhauser high compression heads, Thickstun inlet and Stromberg 97 carburettors. This period piece sees plenty of active use, including the drag strip.

INSET: The potent and stylish turbocharged Sierra Cosworth. Powered by a 2-litre, 16 valve, twin-cam, fuel injected Ford/Cosworth engine, the car is a direct spin-off of Ford's return to Grand Prix racing. The body/chassis was developed by Ford Special Vehicle Engineering and features a characteristic rear spoiler, bonnet louvres and air intake. The maximum speed is around 150 mph and the 0-60 time around 6.5 seconds. Rally prepared versions have a 0-60 time of about 4.5 seconds (courtesy Ford Motor Company).

This re-creation of an early Lakes-style Roadster was built by Brian Lucas using a 1932 chassis with an imported American fibre-glass Roadster body. A 1946 Ford supplied the back axle, shocks, brakes and a number of other parts. The chassis was heavily reworked and now includes a Model A front crossmember to lower the car further. The engine is a 24-stud 239 ci Mercury 59A unit, fitted with Edelbrock heads and fed by triple carburettors and an Offenhauser inlet manifold. A classic piece!

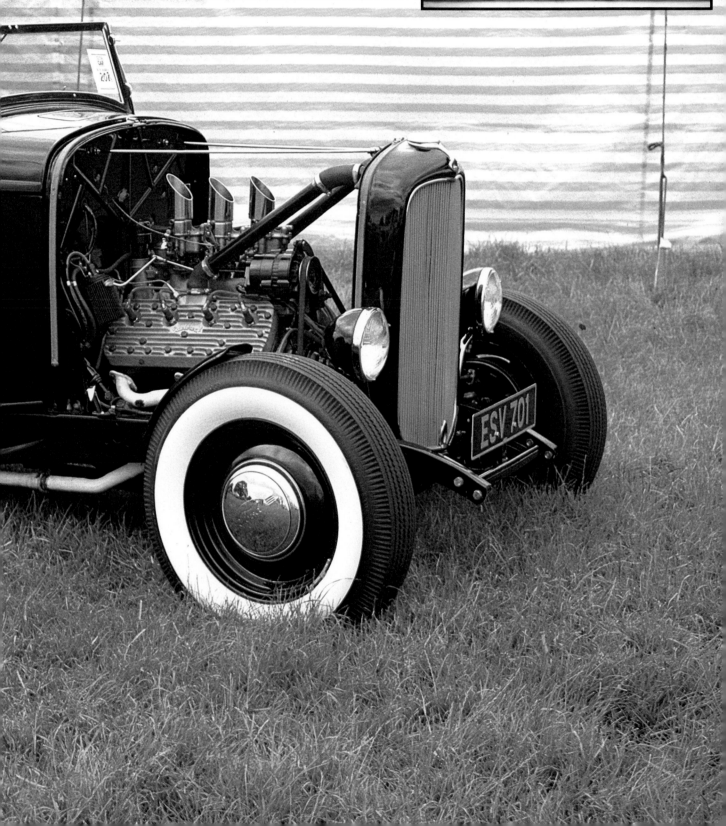

INSET: An example of a "Competition Altered" drag car built and raced by Graham Peake. It features a heavily modified Model T body and is powered by a hot RS 2000 motor. The transmission is via a clutch operated BW 35 autobox, modified for manual operation. The rear axle is a much-narrowed Austin Westminster unit. Typical quarter mile times are in the region of 11.5 seconds with terminal speeds of 120 mph. Less potent street-driven versions also exist!

A unique example of a Briggs-bodied Model A Sedan built by John Cross. The Briggs body is unusual in that it lacks the rear side windows and is four inches wider than the standard body. A Haig chassis was used, this having an independent front and rear suspension. The extensive restoration of the body included a roof chop and louvre-less bonnet sides, as well as complete replacement of the wooden framing. Power is provided by a Rover V8 with autobox. The low stance, single colour paint scheme, Connolly hide interior and chrome wire wheels complete the look.

A resto-style Model A Roadster. Underneath its classic lines is a reproduction chassis and modern drive-train. The interest and popularity of the Model A has increased greatly in recent years, largely as a result of the appearance of high quality fibre-glass bodies and reproduction chassis. Many, such as the car shown here, opt for the semi-restoration look.

An example of a chopped reproduction Model A Sedan Delivery recently brought onto the British market. The styling reflects the contemporary high-tech, one-piece look currently finding favour in both Britain and America. This type of "kit rod" makes a good starting point and can be fitted with a variety of drive-trains. This particular example is powered by a four-cylinder Ford engine. Notice the use of rectangular headlights, horizontal grill slats and low stance, giving the car its distinctive look.

A fine pair of Model Ys. One is based on a reproduction chassis and powered by a Ford 2-litre OHC engine with BW 35 autobox. The front suspension came from an HB Viva, whilst the rear consists of a GT Cortina axle mounted on XJ6 coil-overs and located with a four-bar system. The other car retains an original chassis, suitably strengthened by the addition of boxing and extra cross-members. Its impressive performance comes as a result of a Ford 3-litre V6 mated to a Rover five-speed manual gearbox. The rear suspension is a Jaguar IRS. Both cars retain their steel bodywork with the exception of wider fibre-glass front and rear wings.

INSET: The Model B Sedan Delivery, although very scarce, has always been popular with rodders. This chopped reproduction version was built by Kim Leonard of Bedfordshire and is based on a Jago fibre-glass body and reproduction chassis. Providing the power is the ever-popular Rover V8 backed up by a BW 35 autobox. The rear suspension is from an S-type Jaguar and the front from a Mk III Cortina. Chrome wire wheels and low stance complete the classic look.

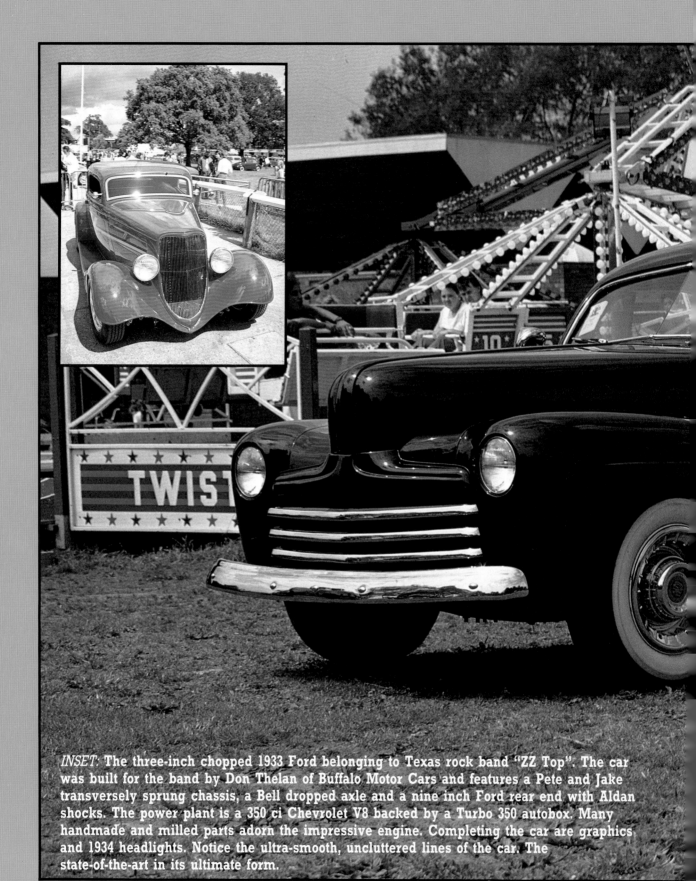

INSET: The three-inch chopped 1933 Ford belonging to Texas rock band "ZZ Top". The car was built for the band by Don Thelan of Buffalo Motor Cars and features a Pete and Jake transversely sprung chassis, a Bell dropped axle and a nine inch Ford rear end with Aldan shocks. The power plant is a 350 ci Chevrolet V8 backed by a Turbo 350 autobox. Many handmade and milled parts adorn the impressive engine. Completing the car are graphics and 1934 headlights. Notice the ultra-smooth, uncluttered lines of the car. The state-of-the-art in its ultimate form.

This classic custom was based on a 1947 American Business Coupe. The car was recently imported from America where most of the work had been carried out. The top had been skilfully chopped and flowed into the body. As well as a severe lowering, the body has been cleaned of seams, handles, badges and ornamentation. The side trim came from an early Buick and the hub caps from a Cadillac. The power plant is a Chevrolet V8 with an autobox. The solid black paint scheme helps to accentuate the car's long, low lines. A period classic!

The Prefect has been a fairly uncommon rod up to recent years. This 2000 V4-powered version was constructed by Geoff Harris, of Cheltenham, and was one of the later models with the scaled-down Pilot grill. Backing up the V4 is a 2000 E gearbox. The front suspension came from an SL90 Viva and the rear from a Jaguar. Notice the use of louvres and the Popular rear wings, widened by six inches. The heavy rake plus lack of bumpers, helps to give the car a "mean" look.

CHAPTER FOUR

Pre-war days

This era saw the arrival of what was to become the most loved and sought after car for a rod-building project. The Model B and its V8-powered brother, the 18, were for many years the ultimate car for a rodder to own or build. Although the production run was fairly brief, a surprising number managed to survive in America. A range of different body styles was available including a roadster, phaeton, coupes and two and four-door sedans. The initial interest centred around the roadster and three-window coupe but as available supplies dried up, rodders gradually turned their attention to other models, such as the sedans.

In recent years, even in America, it has become increasingly difficult to turn up a good steel Model B body, the result being that a whole range of glass bodies has become widely available. Many of these are surprisingly authentic and when equipped with the appropriate accessories and trim parts, are difficult to distinguish from the real thing. Britain had few Model Bs to begin with, although production

carried on up to 1935. The Model 18, with its V8, was scarcer still. Apart from depletion due to the natural ravages of time, the B/18 suffered badly at the hands of "stock-car" racers of the 50s. Because of their advantageous power:weight ratio, they formed an easy way to go stock-car racing, requiring little modification apart from stripping off the wings and gutting the interior. Many otherwise saveable Bs and 18s tragically met their fate in this way.

The result, in Britain, has meant that, with a few exceptions, Model Bs are based on glass-bodied cars. A number of domestic glass bodies have been available for some years but, as with the A, authenticity and finish has sometimes been very poor. Once again, the American bodies have generally been of a much better quality, but importation costs are obviously high.

There are a relatively small number of steel-bodied Dagenham-built Model Bs on Britain's roads today plus a few others imported from America. There are a number of styling differences between the British and American-produced Bs, the general consensus of opinion being that the American cars, with their more rounded lines, are more desirable. Despite this, no rodder worth his salt would turn down the chance of owning a B, whatever its origins! It goes without saying that the cost of building either a steel or glass Model B-based rod can be very high indeed!

The car, that in the early 30s, saved Ford of Britain from financial disaster was the Dagenham-built Model Y. For a long time these received little or no attention from rodders, however, the last five years has seen a great deal of interest in the little car. As with many British cars, a combination of rain and scrap metal drives has helped to decimate their numbers, although a fair number managed to survive. Because of their relatively small size, it's possible to build a fairly cheap rod around a Model Y. The use of a domestic four-cylinder engine and its associated drive-train is an attractive option although Ys have been built with large, supercharged V8s squeezed into their small engine bays.

Reproduction chassis and glass bodies have recently become available although the majority of British built Ys have retained, at least in part, their steel bodies.

The American successor to the Model B/18, was the very attractive Model 40. Rather surprisingly, for a long time, this came second place behind the B in many American rodder's eyes. The last decade has seen a huge increase in the 40s popularity although there are very few in Britain. The only option for the wealthy rodder is to import one, consequently they are very uncommon. British-made repros are slowly becoming available and this will undoubtedly boost their popularity in the future.

The British-built pre-war cars have always been well-liked by rodders although, as with many other models, these have become increasingly scarce. There are a number of rodded examples of the Ford 8 and 10 in Britain, although they are not common. It has become increasingly easy to rod some of these pre-war "uprights" as a number of reproduction parts produced for the later 103E Populars will interchange with these similarly designed cars. Other cars of the period, such as the Model C Deluxe and the 62, have been rodded in even smaller numbers, availability, once again, being the main problem.

Right:
The classic hot rod! This chopped Model B three-window Coupe exhibits a mixture of resto and drag styles. The front suspension is based around a drop-tube set-up whilst the rear uses an IRS. The wheels are American chromed wires. Power for this sophisticated rod comes from an exotically carburated American V8. Note the neat little "nerf" bars at the front.

Left:

The Model B Sedan Delivery, although very scarce, has always been popular with rodders. This chopped reproduction version was built by Kim Leonard of Bedfordshire and is based on a Jago fibre-glass body and reproduction chassis. Providing the power is the ever-popular Rover V8 backed up by a BW 35 autobox. The rear suspension is from an S-type Jaguar and the front from a Mk III Cortina. Chrome wire wheels and low stance complete the classic look.

Below:

This "low boy" has been loosely based on a Model B Roadster. Its styling is

CUSTOM fords

descended from the early lakes and oval track racers. Its exceptionally clean lines are enhanced by the lack of louvres, hinges, badges, handles and the "hidden" number plate. The front suspension consists of a drop-tube mounted on coil-overs and located by a four-bar system. Unlike its American counterpart, this British car has wings covering its skinny steel wheels.

Above: There is no doubt where this influence came from, the drag racing look being obvious. This repro Model B, built by Hugh Hanchard, is definitely "down-in-the-weeds" and has also been heavily chopped. The power is provided by a Ford 351 ci V8 complete with GMC 6-71 supercharger. The gearbox is a four-speed manual and the rear axle, a much-narrowed 9 inch Ford unit fitted with Volvo discs, Spax coil-overs and located with a four-bar system. The low stance was achieved by the use of a 6.5 inch drop-tube front axle mounted on a transverse spring. The backbone for the project was a set of modified Deuce Factory frame rails.

Below: A recent "state-of-the-art" Roadster showing a great deal of American influence. Notice the clean, uncluttered lines of the fibre-glass body. The use of a drop-tube front axle, high-tech wheels, graphic paintwork and lack of wings add to the US look. Motive power comes courtesy of a low slung Ford "Cologne" V6, not the more traditional V8. This is one of the cleanest Roadsters to appear on the British scene in recent years.

Below: This British 4-door Model B could almost pass, with the exception of the wheels, as a superb restoration. Underneath is a modern drive-train complete with Rover V8 power, the rest of the running gear largely consisting of Jaguar components, this including a narrowed IRS. The steering box is a VW item. Externally, the only alteration is a Model A "dropped" headlight bar. Rodders often prefer 2-door to 4-door models however clearly the latter can form the basis of a good looking rod.

Above The American Model 40 has increased in popularity in recent years, although problems of cost and availability have limited their numbers on British roads. Formerly, they were less favoured than the Model B however the situation has now reversed and their sleek, racey lines are now in demand in both steel and reproduction form. With its chopped top, low stance and louvre-less bonnet sides, this car shows the current 1980s trend towards low, smooth rods.

This reproduction Model B Roadster has been given a 1950s theme. With period touches such as Moon discs, flames and louvres, the car would have looked at home racing across the lake beds. A distinguishing feature that identifies it from an original early rod is the use of modern components such as radial tyres and a four-bar front suspension system.

Above: It took Reudi Bartholdi no less than six years to construct his, ultra-low, 1938, Ford 8. The car was based on a 2x3 inch tube chassis that now houses a 327 ci small block Chevrolet V8 producing about 350 bhp. The power is transmitted via a Muncie M21 four-speed box to a narrowed 9 inch Ford rear axle suspended by coil-overs and located by a four bar system and Panhard rod. The immaculate body was treated to a 2.5 inch roof chop and 112 louvres in the bonnet. The wide rear wheels have been successfully kept under standard width arches. The interior houses a full roll cage, clearly showing the drag racing influence. The car was caught in action at Santa Pod Raceway.

Below:
This 1939 Model is a scarce import from America and retains most of its original body features and trim. Stance and stamped aluminium wheels are reminiscent of the American drag racers of the 1960s.

Facing page, Bottom:
The distinguishing single grill opening differentiates the 8 from the more common Popular. This example has been built in a semi-resto style. It's not a common car in rodded guise, however, many of the reproduction parts and panels, such as wings, for the Popular, will interchange with the 8. The rodding of the 8 generally follows a similar pattern to that of the Popular, use often being made of four-cylinder Ford engines.

Above:

With the exception of wheels, sun-roof and VW indicators, this 1936 two-door Model Y, built by Bob Vickers, would be a credit to any restorer. The bonnet side bulge adds necessary clearance for the Lotus twin-cam engine, an unusual choice for a rod.

Right:

This two-door model Y retains most of its original trim with the exception of the bumpers. With stylish chromed wire wheels and meticulously restored bodywork, it clearly shows the resto theme. The appearance of reproduction fibre-glass panels, such as wings and running boards, as well as complete chassis, has made the rodding of the Y much easier in recent years. Surprisingly, the little cars were largely ignored by rodders until the 1970s.

This drag/resto styled Model Y packs a punch courtesy of a supercharged Rover V8. Superchargers have always been popular with rodders in both America and Britain. It's quite remarkable what some rodders manage to squeeze into such a small engine bay! Not surprisingly, the performance is impressive.

Facing page; Top:

With solid bonnet sides, chopped top and steel wheels with trim rings, this Model Y reflects the rodding styles of the 50s and early 60s. Notice the Y's similarity to the larger American Model 40. The latter was a scaled-up version of the Y built for the American market.

Facing page, Bottom:

This rare all-steel, four-door Model Y, of Tony Ham, was based on an original chassis, suitably boxed and with extra cross-members. The power plant is a hot 273 ci V8 from a 1957 Chevrolet, backed up by a Muncie four-speed box. Not surprisingly, this combination was a very tight fit! The front suspension consists of a 1936 V8 I-beam axle, steering box and transverse spring. The rear suspension is a Jaguar IRS narrowed by an astonishing sixteen inches each side! The Jade Green body has been punched with over 300 louvres.

CUSTOM *fords*

Below:

A fine pair of Model Ys. The one is based on a reproduction chassis and powered by a Ford 2-litre OHC engine with BW 35 autobox. The front suspension came from an HB Viva, whilst the rear consists of a GT Cortina axle mounted on XJ6 coil-overs and located with a four-bar system. The wheels are Keystone double wires. The other car retains an original chassis, suitably strengthened by the addition of boxing and extra cross-members. Its impressive performance comes as a result of a Ford 3-litre V6 mated to a Rover five-speed manual gearbox. The rear suspension is a Jaguar IRS. Both cars retain their steel bodywork with the exception of wider fibre-glass front and rear wings.

domestic Ford engines, both OHV and OHC, have been fitted with comparative ease. With moderate increases in horsepower, the retention of the original chassis is a distinct possibility, although in many cases, this is strengthened by the addition of boxing, reinforcing plates and extra cross-members. Engines taken from the later Cortina, Capri and Escort ranges

CHAPTER FIVE

Times of change

This 1940 Deluxe American model has been lowered, de-bumpered and fitted with Moon discs thus giving it a flavour reminiscent of the 1950s. The running gear is largely as Henry made it. Unfortunately few of these cars ever found their way here, being totally unsuitable for the more conservative and modest requirements of the British market.

The 40s and 50s were, despite a World War, a busy and productive period for both Ford of Britain and America. A large number of new cars appeared as well as a number of model ranges that were to last, with various updates, for many years.

Of the cars of this period, the pre-war British models, such as the E04A Anglia and E93A Prefect, have always been sought after by rodders despite their overall similarity to the later and much more available 103E Populars. The modifying of these models has become a fairly straightforward operation, as during the last five to ten years a wide variety of interchangeable mechanical and body parts has been produced for the 103E Popular. This has meant that reproduction chassis, fibre-glass body panels and a variety of trim parts has made the modifying of these cars a relatively painless operation. In the majority of cases, the infamous transverse springing system is the first thing that is replaced, shortly followed by the four-cylinder side-valve and its associated drive-train. More modern

Above:

This V8 Pilot, apart from wide chrome wheels, could easily pass as a restoration. Whereas some early rodders caused a lot of damage to many cars, today's show a great appreciation of Fords original sheet metal.

are popular choices for transplanting. The E93A Prefect has, until recently, been less favoured, mainly because of its four doors, rodders generally preferring two-door models.

1947 saw the introduction of what was to become a perennial favourite, in the shape of the V8-powered Pilot. Initially, this was powered by a choice of either a 2.5 or 3.6 litre V8, although the smaller option was soon discontinued. In rodding terms, the Pilot has always been a car that does not need a great deal of modification. The V8 responds well to the many tried and trusted tuning techniques and even in its standard form, will produce quite respectable performance. Consequently, it is not uncommon to come across pilots that have been tastefully painted and trimmed and fitted with custom wheels, but are still essentially standard in mechanical terms. Having said that, there are plenty of engine bays chock full of modern OHV V8s! The bodywork, which can be traced directly back to the Model 62, is rarely modified to any large degree, most rodders being content to leave its stately lines alone.

The Mk I Consul, Zephyr and later, Zodiac, were something of a breakaway for Ford and caused a sensation in the motoring world on their first appearance. The cars were an immediate success and even today, still have plenty of admirers. These cars were some of the first British Fords destined to be modified in a variety of different ways. Amongst other things, the Mk Is were some of the earliest British Fords to be customised. This initially took the form of an over abundance of accessories and extras, but in later years, examples began to emerge with smoothed-in front and rear-ends, fender skirts, custom grills and severe lowering jobs. A number of these retained the original engines but many more were treated to a transplant. Ford V8s of American origin were a popular choice. Apart from the custom styles, Mk Is were re-worked in the style of the drag strip. This usually involved the skinny front and large rear wheel/tyre combination. Some of the most successfully restyled cars managed to keep this additional rubber tucked neatly under standard width arches, courtesy of narrowed rear axles. The Mk I range was one of the first to cross the divide between the British rodding and custom camps and as such, was to set certain trends that many later cars were to follow.

Below and bottom of facing page: **This classic custom was based on a 1947 American Business Coupe. The car was recently imported from America where most of the work had been carried out. The top has been skilfully chopped and flowed into the body. As well as a severe lowering, the body has been cleaned of seams, handles, badges and ornamentation. The side-trim came from an early Buick and the hub caps from a Cadillac. The power plant is a Chevrolet V8 with an autobox. The solid black paint scheme helps to accentuate the car's long, low lines. A period classic!**

Below:
A typically rodded Pilot, retaining stock bodywork. The only obvious alterations are motorcycle front indicators, modified headlights and wide chrome wheels. The Pilot was the last factory built British Ford to be powered by the side-valve V8.

CUSTOM *fords*

Above: **The current trend of low suspension, high-tech modular wheels and two-tone paintwork is well reflected in this Pilot. Although comparatively little has been done to alter and update its looks, these few alterations have completely changed its overall character.**

The Prefect has been a fairly uncommon rod up to recent years. This 2000 GT V4-powered version was constructed by Geoff Harris, of Cheltenham, and was one of the later models with the scaled-down Pilot grille. Backing up the V4 is a 2000 E gearbox. The front suspension came from an SL90 Viva and the rear from a Jaguar. Notice the use of louvres and the Popular rear wings, widened by six inches. The heavy rake plus lack of bumpers, helps to give the car a "mean" look.

This V8-powered Prefect has the traditional drag style stance and big rear/skinny front wheel combination. Some clever body working is in evidence as the top has been chopped and the four-door body skilfully converted to a two-door. The graphic paint scheme gives the car a definite 1980s look.

CUSTOM Fords

Inset: **The rear of this super-clean 1953 Prefect, built by Steve Boden, features tunnelled lights, a custom touch dating from the 30s and 40s. The immaculate car is powered by a V4 Corsair motor and, remarkably, was the owner's first attempt at rod building. The use of a live rear axle hung on coil-overs, instead of an IRS unit, aids the overall clean look of the car.**

The mid-50s saw the arrival of the more modestly sized and priced 100E range of cars. Considering the price and availability, it took a surprisingly long time for rodders and customisers to latch onto them. 100Es had been used as the basis for a wide range of automotive projects, from saloon car racing to rallying, throughout the 50s and well into the 60s. Few were customised in the true sense, perhaps because of their comparatively small size. It was the mid to late 60s before they began to appear in substantial numbers, the majority reflecting the influence of the drag strip. Four-cylinder Ford engines were a common transplant although V6 and V8-powered versions appeared in later years. Frequently, the McPherson strut-type front suspension was retained, with struts from a number of later models swapped in. By the end of the decade, the 100E range had firmly established itself with Prefects, Anglias and Populars, as well as the little commercials, being seen in increasing numbers.

The replacement, in 1956, of the Mk I Consul, Zephyr, Zodiac, range by the newly styled Mk IIs, gave the British motorist a car that would have looked equally at home in America. The Mk II range was a natural choice for modifying but, as with the Mk Is, in the early days this tended to take the form of extra trim, lights and aerials, as well as American-styled extras such as white-wall tyres and continental kits. These cars found a lot of friends and still have many today. Once again, the cars formed the basis for both custom projects and later, as drag race clone cars. On the custom side, cars were built using the styles and techniques that had been pioneered in America, decades

The first 103E Popular to be turned into a Coupe, by Paul Kempton. A huge amount of body-working skill went into the conversion of a standard saloon body into the coupe, a style to which the British market was never treated. Note the use of the three-slot Ford 10 grille shell, always a favourite with rodders. Power is now provided by a 3-litre Ford V6.

Right:
Built by Nick Lang, this black 1954 Popular features a home-built box-section chassis, now housing a 3-litre V6 with a C4 autobox. The rear suspension is from an S-type Jaguar and the front, from a Triumph Vitesse. The use of steel wheels fitted with Moon discs gives the car a 1950s look, although the fibre-glass panels, low stance and sophisticated interior mean that it could only be a much later car.

Above:
A super-clean example of a 1980s Popular. Bodily, the car remains standard with the exception of fibre-glass front and rear wings. The appearance of fibre-glass panels in recent years has made life much easier for the would-be rodder, as the supply of good steel ones dried up many years ago.

Above:
This chopped
Popular of John Heaney,
is typical of the current crop of
high quality street-rods. The top features a steel
insert, instead of the fabric panel, this aiding the
overall smooth look. Power comes courtesy of a
Rover V8 and autobox. A suitably strengthened
original chassis was used, this now housing
Vauxhall front suspension and a narrowed
live rear axle.

Centre feature:
This V8-powered Popular, built
by Tony Jarvis, has a flip-body
a la "Funny Car" but its low
stance also gives it something
of the look of the early lakes
racers. To achieve this look,
the body was widened by six
inches, channelled by five
inches and the wheel base
elongated! Motive power
comes from a hot Rover V8
with a BW 35 autobox. The
front axle is a stainless steel
drop-tube item and the rear, an
XJ6 Jaguar unit. This is an
excellent and ingenious
treatment of Britain's favourite
street-rod.

before. Tops were chopped, fender skirts added and custom front and rear ends constructed. There were many cars that were mildly modified, often adding two-tone paint with a few body modifications, but falling short of the expensive and difficult roof-chop. Other examples followed the look of the drag strip, with hood-scoops, balloon rear tyres, full roll-cages, gutted interiors and frequently, a large V8 of American origin under the bonnet. As with the customs, many milder versions were constructed, some combining trends and styling components from both.

Throughout this period, Ford were churning out the, near-obsolete, car that was to ultimately form the backbone of the British rodding scene, the antiquated 103E Popular. These proved to be aptly named and during the years following their demise, became the most widely modified British Ford. Cars were built with an enormous range of power-plants, from hotted-up four-cylinder side-valves, up to V6, V8 and even V12s. The most popular four-cylinders were Ford OHV and OHC engines in their various guises and the most popular V8, the domestic Rover engine. As their popularity spread, so did the availability of reproduction parts, this leading to even further increases in their numbers. Suffice it to say, that if the humble 103E had not been adapted in such great numbers, the rodding scene in Britain would probably be about one third its current size! The 103E had provided rodders with a springboard for their immensely imaginative ideas, the result being an amazing potpourri of styles. Without the Popular, many people would never have become involved in rodding.

In retrospect, this period covering these two decades gave birth to a number of cars that were to form the bedrock of the British rod and custom scene.

Photographs on facing page:

Top:
This step-side pick-up conversion was based on a conventional Saloon, and was built by aircraft engineer, Steve Woodley. The chassis was lengthened by fourteen inches and the front half of the body turned into the cab. All of the compound curves involved in the metalwork were made by the owner. He was also responsible for moulding the rear fibre-glass arches and building the aluminium/wood bed. The Ford V6 that provides the power, features many hand-made aluminium and stainless steel components. Likewise, the Jaguar IRS also has many unique touches. The end result is very stylish. What a pity Ford never made one!

Centre:
This 1938 Fordson van was originally built by Robyn Slater and later updated by Alistair Papworth. It features a home-built box-section chassis that houses a 2.5 litre Daimler V8 and BW 35 autobox. The motor is fed from a Mazda four barrel carburettor. The front suspension is Vauxhall Viva fitted with Victor discs and Spax shock absorbers. The rear suspension is an S-type Jaguar IRS, narrowed seven inches each side and fitted with Triumph Herald coil-overs. The body was chopped three inches, fitted with steel Prefect arches, a two slot grill and punched full of louvres. These little commercials have always been popular with rodders although there are relatively few survivors.

Bottom: **Yet another example of the ubiquitous Popular, this time with a difference. The two-seater convertible conversion had been superbly carried out by Russ White using a boxed chassis and a 1957 body. As an additional styling exercise, the boot lid had been punched full of louvres. The front suspension is an HA Viva unit with Kawasaki 1000 motorcycle springs and the rear, an S-type Jaguar IRS. The engine is now a 3-litre V6 and autobox from a Granada.**

Above:
There's no missing this street-driven/drag raced Fordson van of Bob Swansborough. The little commercial packs a mighty punch courtesy of a nitrous-injected, supercharged 454 ci Chevrolet V8. Its flawless black bodywork is complemented by the 1980s style graphic paint scheme.

Left:
This Popular features reverse air intakes in the bonnet sides and blacked out chromework. It's very much a car of the 1980s and reflects the trend towards "low profile" subtle changes. This is opposed to an over abundance of chrome and garish paint schemes that were in fashion during the late 60s and early 70s.

Facing page, centre:
This Mk I Consul has had only minimal body modifications but when coupled with a tasteful single colour paint scheme, the overall appearance has been subtly changed. The clean look is aided by the lack of badges and over-riders. Although now becoming relatively scarce, these cars can still form the basis of a fairly inexpensive way to get into rodding/customising.

CUSTOM *Fords*

This heavily modified Fordson van reflects the trend towards circuit racing styles. The styling is reminiscent of some of the 1960s Saloon car racers although engineering and bodywork is far superior to those early cars. This little van runs four-cylinder Ford power.

Despite the lack of major body modificatons, the drag styling is quite evident with this Mk I Zephyr. Powered by a 302 ci Ford V8, the car features wide rear tyres tucked under standard arches. It is always especially rewarding to see such potent "old" cars in action. This one was caught racing at Santa Pod.

Below: **This is what a "British custom" of the 1950s looked like. This Zodiac has been beautifully restored, both cosmetically and mechanically, and "accessorised" in the style of the post-war era. It represents a sort of half-way house between restoration and customising.**

Above:

The headlight peaks, sun visor and standard wheels with white-walls and spinners gives this Mk I Consul a late 1950s custom style. Many of the cars built during this period retained most of the original mechanical parts. At the time, few accessories and tuning parts were available consequently most modifications were home-built.

CUSTOM Fords

Left:
The 100E Prefect is less commonly customised than its 2-door counterparts, however, this one still makes a nice semi-resto custom. Apart from immaculate bodywork, it sports chrome wire wheels and a visor. A major problem when modifying 100Es is the lack of both steel and fibre-glass body panels. On the positive side, OHV engines can easily be fitted using 107E cross members. The front struts from the larger Classic can also be fitted, giving both uprated suspension and disc brakes.

Below left: **This is what is termed a "street sleeper". At first glance this Mk I Consul appears to be virtually unaltered apart from the addition of headlight peaks and wheel trims. The immaculate bodywork, subtle paint finish and low stance fail to reveal that under the bonnet resides a Ford V6 with performance to match!**

Left:

A 1961 100E Popular with a number of post-war American custom ideas. The flamed paint, lake pipes and bobbed rear wings were popular touches during the 1960s. The grill insert is from a Rover 3500 and much of the interior from a Mk I Escort. A 1500 Cortina engine and gearbox provides the power, the rear axle also coming from the same source.

Right:
These little vans have become popular in recent years. Although largely standard in its bodywork, this 1959 Thames of Ian Webb has been lowered and de-bumpered. It is powered by a hot 1500 GT Ford engine coupled to a 2000E gearbox. The rear axle is a narrowed Cortina unit. Notice the nicely tunnelled rear lights.

Below:
A former drag car returned to the street. This 100E Popular was constructed from a part-built drag car and was originally intended to run in the "Street" classes, using a turbocharged 1500 Ford engine. It was rebuilt using Mk II Escort front suspension, 1500 GT engine, Anglia gearbox and Cortina rear axle mounted on 100E springs. The car also featured a tilt-front, Peugeot grille and Triumph 1300 steering column. Note the wide alloy wheels have been kept under the standard width arches.

Above:
This van features a number of custom touches more often found on Saloon versions. The front end has been smoothed out, the bonnet louvred, the suspension lowered and a visor added.

Left: **The competition look is reflected in this 1957 300E Thames van built by Ian Armstrong. The immaculate bodywork has been fitted with an Anglia grille and painted Conifer Green. The engine is a 1600 cc cross-flow Ford, from a Mk III Cortina, brought up to GT specification. The rear axle, from a Zodiac, has been narrowed by about seven inches, and is hung on Jaguar S-type dampers with XJ6 springs. Vortex wheels complete the racing look. It couldn't be anything but British.**

Above:

This Mk II Zodiac, built by
Kevin Rooney, has been given
a long, sleek, custom look.
Subtle lowering, slightly flared
rear arches, continental kit and
white upholstery gives a 1950s
theme. Power originally came
from a Daimler V8 although
this was later switched to a
Rover unit. The car was badly
damaged when a propshaft
joint disintegrated, smashing
the floor, gearbox and radiator.
Clearly, it was soon rebuilt to
its former high standard.

Centre:

This 1961 Zephyr of Peter
Brock, is an interesting
mixture of restoration and
custom. The bodywork has
well executed Mirra-Flake
paintwork but is otherwise
standard. Under the bonnet,
power is still provided by the
original straight six which has
been suitably hotted-up by the
addition of a triple SU
carburation set-up and
meticulous detailing. The
owner's attention to detail
throughout the car is apparent.

Right: This fully customised
Mk II features chopped top and
cleaned-up body lines. It also
sports a custom tube grille, as
well as "rolled" front and rear
valances. The entire car has
been built using all of the
classic American custom
techniques, the result being
that it looks much longer and
lower than a stocker.

Right: **With the exception of the five-spoke wheels, this Zodiac could pass as a well kept original. Underneath the excellent sheet metal is a different story, with an updated drive train, powered by a 302 ci Ford V8.**

Below: **This started life as a Zodiac Saloon but has been transformed into a Sedan Delivery. The high riding stance, scoop and tilt-front makes drag styling quite evident. Power comes from a Rover V8 coupled to a five-speed manual gearbox. The conversion involved cutting off the roof from the belt line upwards, welding shut the bottom halves of the rear doors and grafting on sections from a second Zodiac. The rear door now hinges upwards. The rear suspension is Jaguar and the front, a narrowed Transit axle on leaf springs.**

CHAPTER SIX

The 1960s onwards

The period between 1960 and 1980 saw the arrival of a number of new models, the life span of some being very brief. Others appeared that were to be the forerunners of model ranges destined to continue over both decades.

The early part of this era saw a large number of 105E Anglias on the roads. At the time, many of these were modified, mainly in the guise of rally cars. The 997 cc powered version was followed by a 1200 cc model although a frequent engine transplant of the time, was the 1340 cc Classic engine. These cars were largely ignored until the appearance, in the late 1960s, of a number of customised versions. Unfortunately, the custom touches often included a mixture of garish paint schemes, coupled with bulky flared arches and large hood scoops. This combination helped to destroy the Anglia's distinctive lines. After this initial outburst, the Anglia virtually disappeared from the custom scene, only to emerge some years later. The cars that appeared during the 1970s looked a completely different breed. The bulky

Above:
This 105E Anglia features many subtle additions. A Capri "power bulge" has been added to the bonnet and the lower aprons carefully blended in. The wheel arches have been neatly flared and an additional set of rear lights grafted on. The power is provided by a 1500 GT Ford engine. The car abounds with clever ideas and well executed touches.

Facing page:
This Anglia van has formed the basis of a good econo-custom. Loud flames, wide steel wheels and stripped off front gives an early 1960s look. Anglia vans are now fairly rare and it is unusual to come across a customised version.

rally-orientated wheel arches had given way to subtle flares, or even none at all, wide tyres being kept under standard width arches. Over-complex paintwork was replaced by single colours, the result being a surprisingly good looking car. The number customised is still comparatively small although today's 105Es are generally well built and nicely finished.

Of the other cars in this period, perhaps the most stylish to emerge was the Classic Capri. Its sleek, slinky lines made it a natural base for a custom car. With a few simple touches such as de-badgeing, lowering, and fitting with a good set of wheels, the car could be made to look an absolute knockout. The addition of a continental kit, white upholstery and wire wheels, resulted in a clàssic example of a 1960's custom. Mechanically, it was not uncommon for cars to be left as standard, although it was a comparatively simple matter to swap engines from other Ford models. Although a few were treated to the drag strip look, they did not respond well, looking much more effective as low,

smooth, street-cruisers.

The Mk III and IV Consul, Zephyr and Zodiac ranges appeared during this period, however these never assumed a prominent role in either a custom or drag strip role. The distinctive American looks of the Mk II range were not to be repeated, their replacements, by and large, being left unmodified. A few have been mildly customised although this normally entails no more than altered paintwork and a set of after-market wheels. It's surprising what a difference these simple changes can make, the resultant cars being quite pleasing to the eye.

The 1960s saw the first appearance of the ubiquitous Cortina. The Mk I models could easily be improved by the simple addition of wheels, new paintwork and the removal of badges and motifs. It was uncommon to find extensive body modifications, the majority tending to be lowered and fitted with spoilers, giving something of the circuit-racer look. Others were built with the drag strip in mind having raised back ends and the obligatory large rear wheels. A variety of power-plants were to be found under the bonnets, including a large number of Ford V6 engines as well as a smattering of both British and American V8s.

The Mk II version later replaced the Mk I. Only very few were customised, unlike its successor in turn, the Mk III. These were adopted in large numbers by the younger generation in large numbers and customised, with varying degrees of success. The quality of construction varied enormously. At the lower end, they were ''over-accessorised'' and treated to an assortment of poor quality panels. At the other, there were Mk IIIs of excellent quality, with well fitting extra panels, high-tech modular wheels and subtle, well

executed paintwork. With the passage of time, the rougher cars disappeared leaving their better built successors.

Of the Mk IV/V range the majority tended to be modified by engine transplants or by the body styling kit route.

Ford's ever-popular Escort range was never as popular as the Cortinas for customising, perhaps because their smaller size did not respond as successfully as their larger brethren. The earlier Escorts suffered the same fate as the Cortina, often being heavily "over-accessorised". Later years saw a distinct improvement with the arrival of the Mk II and well fitting X-pack arches and additional panels. These cars were comparatively few in number, the majority of Escorts being more heavily influenced by the rally scene. When treated to the drag strip look, perhaps because of their size, many cars tended to look very ungainly as a result of the severe rake that many suffered. Generally, the Escort range did not look its best in the guise of a drag strip racer.

In the late 1960s the Capri was launched and with its "sporty" looks immediately found favour with the younger generation. As with the Cortina, the earliest cars were generally greatly over done. As the range matured so did the ideas and techniques of their owners. Later cars reflected the improved looks and qualities of additional panels as the body styling trend became established.

Mk III Zephyrs were not often used for custom projects, but the addition of a good paint scheme and a set of alloy wheels makes a dramatic improvement, even to a stocker.

CUSTOM Fords

Left:

An example of a tastefully customised early Capri, clearly showing the trans-Atlantic styling of the times. Although the body changes are minimal, the overall effect is very successful. The car sports chrome wire wheels with white-walls and features a simple white paint scheme. The rear is finished off with a beautifully constructed continental kit made from sections of bumper. The interior has a 1960s feel about it, with white tuck and roll upholstery. The overall effect of these changes is to make the car look long, low and slippery. Undoubtedly one of the most stylish Fords of the era.

Below:

A modified and now, uncommon Classic. Although not often customised, this mildly reworked example has responded quite successfully to the addition of flames, alloy wheels and a tidied up front end. The 1340 cc engine was fairly torquey and was a popular swap for 105E Anglias.

Right:
This Mk I Cortina features dramatically restyled front end. The grille has been panelled in, the lower apron blended and air openings added to the bonnet. The design shows some similarities to that adopted for the mid 1980s Sierra. An interesting treatment to an old favourite.

Facing page; Top:
Rather surprisingly Escorts were not as commonly customised as might be expected. The majority that were customised were usually based on the Mk I, Mk II versions being relatively rare. In both cases, mechanical modifications were often minimal, most of the alterations being cosmetic. This usually took the form of additions rather than sheet metal alterations. This typical example features fat arches, spoiler and rear window louvres.

Right:
A refreshing and an unusual combination. This Escort van has been treated to an RS2000-look, making use of an RS front and spoiler. Interestingly, it has also been fitted with a set of modified X-pack arches. A tasteful, single colour paint scheme and alloy wheels finish it off. It is unusual to find a modern commercial vehicle given a performance image, the majority tending to opt for creature comforts and opulent interiors.

Bottom:

This mildly customised Classic Capri has been de-badged and has a cleaned up front end. A slight rake and alloy wheels enhance its already distinctive lines. In retrospect, these were very stylish cars for the times and are only recently beginning to be fully appreciated.

Above:
A clever pick-up conversion
constructed by K. Portsmouth.
The off-road style hauler was
based on a 1970 Mk II Cortina.
The much-modified body now
sits on a home-built
box-section chassis which is
also home for the Ford V6 that
now provides the power. The
front axle is a narrowed
Transit unit, mounted on leaf
springs. With its large wheels
and tyres and high stance, it
manages to look remarkably
like one of the current crop of
Japanese mini-trucks.

Facing page; Bottom:
This Mk I Escort has been
cleverly converted into a
stylish pick-up. The back half
of the roof has been cut off, the
boot area removed and the
remainder converted into the
bed. Note how the original rear
window has been retained
making it look somewhat
similar to a scaled-down El
Camino. Not only does it look
good, it also packs a punch
courtesy of a detailed Ford V6.

Above: **Another pick-up with the "off-road" look, this time a P100. Although not considered to be as such, the off-road look is largely an offshoot of main stream customising. Very few of these vehicles see any off-road service, however, they provide an interesting addition to the street scene and contrast greatly with the current low, sleek custom look.**

The styling of this Mustang owes more to the race circuit than the drag strip. If it didn't look so good it could almost pass for an old NASCAR racer. Most of its predecessors emulated the drag look, with big rear tyres and a heavy rake. The Mustang has had an enormous range of engine options available over the years, so performance has varied greatly from model to model. This one looks a killer!

Left:
An example of a mildly customised Cortina. Modifications include front and rear spoilers, alloy wheels, side-marker lights and two-tone paintwork. Note the slightly raised rear and flared rear arches needed to cover the wide rear wheels.

Centre:
A much modified Mk III GT Cortina. Amongst the many alterations are a custom bonnet, front spoiler and reshaped side windows. The car features a much modified interior and a host of minor modifications as well as the more obvious ones. The styling of the rear wing shows some similarities to that of the "Superbird". The car was used in a major tyre manufacturer's advertising campaign.

Right:
The subtly modified Cortina of David Cockell. The addition of spoilers, side stripes and alloy wheels help to alter the image of the car. Under the bonnet is a 2.8 injected Capri motor. The styling trends that were adopted during the 1980s reflected a much more determined effort to enhance, rather than to extensively modify the car, irrespective of its original lines. Comparatively minor changes, as with this car, can greatly improve the overall appearance.

Left:
A tasteful reworking of a Mk I Capri. Notice the classy touches such as notches for the quad tail pipes, smooth valance and small wheel spats. Side skirts, high-tech wheels and a single colour paint scheme help to give the car a circuit racer look.

Right:
A heavily modified Capri with hardly a panel left unaltered! The car has fat wings, scoop, spoilers, window louvres, graphics, custom grille and "Zoomie" pipes! This reflects what many people consider to be a "custom car", however, true customs usually have pieces removed in order to clean up the lines, as opposed to parts and panels added. Although many would consider this particular car is "over the top", there is no denying that the look still has its devotees. More recently built cars tend to be lower and smoother.

Right:
A mildly modified Capri with alloy wheels, tube grille and smoothed out lower panel. A typical car of the late 1970s. A large number of similarly styled cars were constructed, many of dubious quality. This is one of the better ones, the modifications having been well executed.

CUSTOM *fords*

This Capri features a number of body changes. The grille has been altered and a large air intake added. In addition, the car features flames and running boards. The panelled side windows were popular for a few years. Most of these modifications became less favoured following the advent of the body styling kit.

Below:
A modern example of "professional customising". This conversion has involved the removal of the Capri's roof. A complex, but completely inconspicuous, system of bracing has put back the lost strength, the result being less body flexing than before the conversion. The car also sports extended and modified RS arches and sill extensions. The wheels are now 7x15 RS items. A very stylish conversion, aptly named the "Capriolet". Mechanically the car is unaltered, a standard 2.8i Capri engine hiding under the bonnet.

CHAPTER SEVEN

The age of body styling

Customising modern Fords can lead to a number of problems. Firstly the engine. With XRs, 'i's, turbos, Cosworths and so on, whats left? The interior? Normally this is plush, with radios, cassettes, tinted glass, all often standard fitments on most Ford vehicles nowadays. Outside? Low profile tyres, RS wheels, aerodynamic bodies. Just where do you start? Stick-on flames or a jacked-up rear end, Oh no! For many years the odd spoiler or wheel arch to bolt or weld onto Escorts and Cortinas has been around. Recently things have started, and will continue to get, more stylish. The age of body styling has arrived!

One of the first concerns in this field was Kat, a British company that specialises in the conversion of production cars into something just a little different. The driving force behind the company is Simon Saunders, who in the past had worked for firms such as Porsche and Aston Martin. Clearly there was plenty of experience there. Kat currently offers a number of services and can convert the exterior, interior, engine and suspension in order to transform standard Fords into "individual" vehicles. The intention with Kat and the other manufacturers, such as XL Design, Pro-Car engineering, RGA, Fibresports, Kamei etc. is for the additional panels to blend in with the original design, so that the car looks like it had been designed that way and not just had parts bolted onto it.

The majority of the kits are made from hand-laid glass-reinforced plastic (GRP), this giving a high strength, durability and providing an excellent surface for subsequent painting. There is always the option, of course, of a colour mixing system to match the panels to the colour of the car, prior to application.

Right:
Fords own version of "RS" body kits, this time on a non-injection Capri. Note that the panels can be supplied colour matched, and pre-cut, prior to application. There is also the option of fitting such a kit onto a brand new vehicle, prior to purchase.

Below:
2.8i Capri with grille infill, lower front spoiler and light louvres. The panels in this example are made from ABS. Rear polyurethane flexy spoilers can also be added (courtesy Richard Grant).

Left:
A Capri 2.8 injection, with body styling kit comprising bumper clip-ons, front spoiler and side skirts. Note that the panels are clip-ons and hence are supplied pre-cut to avoid filling or bonding (courtesy Richard Grant).

With many of the kits, such as those made by Kat and XL design, the panels are all supplied pre-cut, this normally guaranteeing a really good fit. Where possible, air-dams etc., fit over existing bumpers. This avoids filling or bonding at any stage, the result being that a good quality finish is easily obtainable.

Most of the firms already mentioned will also modify interiors. Leather upholstery is often added, seats re-padded, and even electric windows installed where required.

Modifications to the engine can also be undertaken at the same time. A good example of this is the turbo-charging of the Ford 2.8i engine. An uprated version will include a Garrett turbocharger and intercooler, giving outputs of 200-230 bhp. The power can be increased to 280 bhp with a twin turbo package, utilising a pair of T2 turbos. An advisable addition with this system, is an improved braking system.

Below:

A 2.8i turbo Capri complete with grille infill, compomotive wheels and lower spoiler with integral foglights. The indicators blink through the small louvres and the additional side skirts carry the manufacturer's logo. The turbo addition takes the power output to around 230 bhp with a top speed of about 150 mph

claimed. It is interesting to note that Kat will also modify the interior trim, ie. leather upholstery, piping, carpets and headlining (courtesy Kat).

Inset:

A rear view of the Kat Capri showing infilled rear lights, unusual rear boot spoiler and very distinctive rear under-bumper spoiler/valance. This nine part moulding kit for the Capri is constructed from hand-laid GRP. This is the turbo Capri with the 230 bhp output. A twin turbo option is available boosting the power to around 280 bhp. Walnut instrument panels, full retrims and electric windows and mirrors can also be added if required (courtesy Kat).

Now onto the cars themselves. The Capri is currently a popular car with all of the kit manufacturers, with many attractive packages being available. One of the most striking is produced by a company called Automotive. A quick glance at one of their modified cars and it could be a Ferrari Testarossa, but a closer look reveals a Ford Capri lurking in there somewhere. The kit itself is in hand-laid GRP and alterations from standard include valance, bumper, grill cover, wheel arch extensions, door-cladding panels and running-boards. For a less dramatic effect, but just as noticeable, Richard Grant (RGA) supply a range of kits for Mk II and III Capris. The panels from RGA are made from an acrylonitrile-butadiene-styrene co-polymer (ABS) and include grills, side-skirts and front spoilers. Their rear flexy spoilers are manufactured from a polyurethane foam (PU). To alter the rear panel, it is possible to purchase infil panels sporting such logos as "Injection", "Capri" and "2.8i". Companies, such as Autoplas, can also supply a range of extras, such as rear window visors, roof consoles, dashboards, and instrument pods.

Ford's own "RS" version of a styling kit for the Capri, includes a boot spoiler, extended arches, sills and, of course, the ever-popular RS wheels.

Kat's Capri package is perhaps, after Automotive's, one of the most striking examples, especially when teamed up with a Turbo Technics conversion. A typical full conversion of a 2.8i Capri (145 bhp) would involve a nine part moulding kit, Compomotive wheels and a Turbo Technics conversion. A 0-60 time of under six seconds, a top speed of over 150 mph and a power output of around 200 bhp is the result! The designer, Simon Saunders, had previously worked for Tickford and was responsible for the design of their Capri styling set. Tickford subsequently argued that the initial Kat kit was too close to the original design for their liking! As a result, Kat were forced to redesign. Irrespective of which product is chosen, both look equally good!

Now onto the Escort. Many non-XRs have spoilers added, mirrors colour-coded and

additional lights added. From the many kits now available it is possible to upgrade the looks of the 1.1 or 1.3 "Basic" to look like an XR, even if under the bonnet it hasn't quite got the muscle. XL designs can fit any Escort with spoilers, front and back, wheel arch . extensions, side-skirts and door-panels. Deluxe options are also available for twin headlamp conversions and tail grills, the latter being a most striking and subtly blended in item. All modifications keep the standard jacking points although on some, the room for operating the jack is a bit cramped. Are the bumpers and additional panels up to it, if they ever find themselves in a bump? XL are typical of many and quote the following: Front and rear bumpers, 900 gm^2 chopped strand mat plus 200 gm^2 woven roving. Panels, 900 gm^2 chopped strand mat and tail grill about 600 gm^2.

Ford themselves, supply wheel arches, sills and spoilers (as for the Capri) and colour co-ordinated bumpers. To finish the package, their RS wheels are always available. Colour co-ordinated bumpers and side panels are also an option for the Orion range.

RGA supply PU flexy spoilers, tailblazers, infil panels and, perhaps most interesting and noticeable, rear light louvres for the Escort. Kamei and Kat produce kits for Mk III and IV Escorts and Orions, consisting of front spoilers, wheel arch sections and side and rear skirts. Kamei also offer the option of an air scoop. Kat claim that wind-tunnel tests of their Escort have shown that a gain of 5 mph on the top speed is possible. This can be substantially boosted by the addition of a T3 turbo conversion. An XR3i version producing 135 bhp and an RS 1600i version, 140 bhp, gives 0-60 times of around 7 seconds and a top speed in the region of 130-140 mph.

Facing page; Top:

The very striking rear-end of XL Designs' Mk III XR3i Escort. The additional rear light louvres blend in subtly with the rear valance and louvred side skirts. A set of RS wheels add just the right finishing touch. All of the panels in this kit are constructed from 900 gm² chopped strand mat, which would certainly take care of any minor bumps. The exception is the tail grille which is 600 gm². Although this is an XR version, the panels will fit any Mk III three-door saloon or RS, with only minor modifications needed for spoiler fitting to the front of RS versions.

Fitting the kit to an Escort is a straightforward job, as the removal of the over-riders allows the front and rear air-dams to be easily clipped on. Lower panels require fastening around wheel arches with the lamp fillers normally fixing into the old number plate mounting position. One kit that essentially keeps the Escort "look", is the Zender. Their package includes a front spoiler with an integral grill that successfully matches up with the standard Mk III Escort item, plus louvred side-panels adjacent to the rear wheel arches.

The Fiesta seems to have missed the boat as far as body styling kits are concerned, Zender listing one of the few. The Fiesta kit comes complete with a front spoiler, graduated under the grill for effect. Side door-panels, with small louvres cut into them (as for the Escort) can also be added next to the rear wheel arches, as can rear and hatch spoilers. Again, a very fetching car, especially when fitted with RS wheels. Ford's own version has the RS wheels, back

and front spoilers, sills and partial wheel arch covers.

The "old" Mk IV/V Cortina can also have a facelift but again, not as dramatic as the kits available for some of the newer, more aerodynamic Fords. RGA seems to be the main supplier with tailblazers, front and rear spoilers, rear valance and side-lazers. The kits will also fit any of the other Cortina models.

Facing page: Bottom:

For those wanting "minor" modifications, this Mk III four-door Escort is a good example. It has side sills, rear valance, front and rear spoilers and XR-type wheels. It might not have the XR power under the bonnet but it definitely has the looks (courtesy Richard Grant).

Bottom:

A more conservative treatment of a Mk III Escort. Additions include front and rear spoilers, rear valance, side skirts and "lazers". If money is a problem, buying components singly may be a more practical way to enhance the car's looks. (courtesy Richard Grant).

Below:

The Kamei treatment of the Mk III Escort is noted for its distinctive front grille and matching front spoiler. A nice feature is the subtle paintwork additions and side skirts. All Kamei kits are manufactured from impact-resistant, weather-proofed ABS although Kamei's new version "Durokam" is said to be unbreakable and easier for paint application. Other additions can include interesting double bonnet scoops and a host of interior options (courtesy Kamei).

Left:

A Mk III XR3 Escort with the usual Kat treatment of grille infills, side skirts and spoilers, the front being fitted with integral fog lights. This model also has modular wheels. Kat will also fit a turbo and uprated clutch and braking system. An RS turbo version of the Kat Escort can also be produced having a maximum speed of about 140 mph. Interior trim can be modified, together with the addition of new seats and electric windows. There are two types of tailgate spoiler available, a bi-plane floating wing type and a larger high downforce solid type. The former requires filling and respraying of the old mounting points (courtesy Kat).

CUSTOM *fords*

Below:

The Mk IV XR3i Escort with the Kat treatment. Very similar to the Mk III but perhaps a little more stylish, expecially when fitted with RS wheels. As with previous kits all of the parts clip on. Kat claims that, using wind tunnel tests, their kit can increase the typical XR3i Escort top speed by 5 mph. A similar version is available for the Mk II Orion (courtesy Kat).

As with all the other Zender kits, the front spoiler is the eye-catcher. Side skirts, with their distinctive louvres are added. Again RS wheels complete the effect (courtesy Autosport + Design).

Facing page; Top:
This is Formula Design's body styling kit for the Mk IV Escort and XR3i. The similarities between this and the Mk III four-piece kit are quite evident. This kit is fitted to a Mk IV cabriolet XR3i Escort. Notice the use of the latest style, colour co-ordinated, RS wheels (courtesy Formula Design).

Right:
This XR3i features home-modified spoilers, rear panel extensions, and interesting graphic paintwork. This particular example has had all of the "extras" bonded, filled and sprayed to match, something not normally necessary with the professional kits available. When fitted with a T3 turbo 140 bhp can be available and a 0-60 time of around 7 seconds can be achieved.

An example of a 1960s car emulating 1980s styling trends. This Mk I Escort has rear window louvres produced by Autoplas. Other options by the same company include, power intakes, side louvres splatter guards and XR look-a-like wheel covers.

Top:

This is Formula Design's four-piece body styling kit for the Mk III Escort and XR3, designed by Nigel Richards. (Mk IV versions are also available). The front spoiler is a one-piece unit allowing air to be swept down and under the front wheels. Formula Design claim that this kit enables "rock steady handling" at high speeds together with improved drag coefficients. This leads to an improvement in fuel consumption. All the panels can be supplied pre-painted, or factory fitted (courtesy Formula Design).

Centre:

One of the few body styling kits available for the Fiesta, this one supplied by Zender. This model has the attractive "grilled" front spoiler, characteristic of all the Ford/Zender kits. Also added, are side skirts, rear hatch spoiler and rear valance. RS wheels are used to produce a very sporty looking car (courtesy Autosport + Design).

Bottom:

The old favourite, the Cortina, comes in for some treatment. This is one of the few kits (ABS) available and comprises front and rear valance, light infills (tailblazers), flexy rear spoiler (of polyurethane), Compomotive wheels and side sills. All this is packed onto this example of a 1.6 GL Cortina. It is interesting to note that illuminated tailblazers are now available (courtesy Richard Grant).

Now onto the Cortina's replacement, the Sierra. The Zender kit provides skirts and grills and in overall design, matches their Escort and Fiesta kits. The Kat Sierra features a similar range of parts to their Capri. Similarities include indicators blinking through grills (a two-bar grill, in this case) and under-bumper integral fog-lights. One major difference is the Capri air-intake, which remains as standard, unlike the Sierra, which draws in air from the front spoiler, located beneath the bumper. The kit can be adapted for three or five-door versions with interior modifications ranging from minor trim

An eye-catching front spoiler matching the original Sierra grill is part of this body kit by Zender. This kit can be used on both 3 or 5 door versions (courtesy Autosport + Design).

changes to a full Connolly hide retrim. Standard jacking points can be retained, but via panel recesses. Kamei's version for the Sierra is very similar to Ford's own, with sill additions, rear boot spoiler, valance and front spoiler.

There are also turbo conversions available from Turbo Technics for the Sierra, these giving 200, 230 or 280 bhp,

A cheaper form of styling is illustrated on this five-door Sierra Ghia. The additions to the normal Ghia trim include side "lazers" and rear "flexy" spoiler (courtesy Richard Grant).

with speeds of over 160 mph and sub six second 0-60 times claimed.

The Granada, like the Fiesta, has largely been ignored by the kit manufacturers. One of the better examples is that produced for the Mk II Granada by Skeete. Their kit consists of a one-piece front bumper with integral spoiler and grill unit. Side-skirts can be added, together with a rear bumper/spoiler that houses the repositioned number plate. As with many other designs, the parts need no direct bonding to the car. A suspension package is also offered, which lowers the car, uprates the springs and adds adjustable shock absorbers. This clearly improves the overall handling. As far as the styling is

Top:

An all round Kat body kit, similar in design to the Kat Capri, for the three or five-door Sierra. The indicators blink through two-bar louvres. The normal front and rear spoilers and side skirts have been added, the car looking complete with the addition, in this case, of RS wheels. With a turbo conversion, sub six second times are claimed. New wheels, as shown, can be supplied or old ones treated to match or contrast the bodywork (courtesy Kat).

Centre:

An X1 Kamei kit for the Sierra with distinctive side skirts and front and rear spoiler extensions. Not as dramatic as some kits but one of the few companies to retain the original grille. The overall effect is in keeping with the original body style. Kamei claim a higher top speed, improved handling, reduced cross wind effects and better fuel consumption (courtesy Kamei).

Bottom:

The rear of a modified XR4i, this version by Kat. The distinctive rear bi-plane spoiler has been retained and the rear improved by the addition of the number plate infill and rear valance. A choice of three turbo conversions will give a power output of 200-280 bhp and a top speed of around 160 mph. A Connolly hide retrim is also available. Standard jacking points are used via panel recesses (courtesy Kat).

One of the few body styling kits available for the Mk II Granada. This one by Skeete, on a Granada Ghia, adds a one-piece front spoiler with grille infill, together with side skirts and alloy wheels. Skeete will supply the parts or, as with many other companies, can provide a fitting service. The standard jacking points are retained together with the standard wheel/tyre arrangement if required.

The rear view of the Skeete *(below)* Granada showing modified rear bumper with repositioned number plate and Skeete logo. The panels are made from GRP and all of the fixing holes are hidden. The rear bumper/spoiler is a one-piece unit that fits the old number plate fixing position. A suspension package is also offered and consists of four lowered and uprated springs and adjustable shock absorbers, which Skeete claim provide the vehicle with outstanding cornering power and stability (courtesy Skeete).

concerned, the front and rear additions certainly fit in with the original lines of the car. By contemporary standards, the package may look a little dated when compared with the more modern Fords, such as the Mk III Granada, although the Mk II model was undeniably boxy to begin with. This kit definitely helps to improve and update the look of the old Granada. A new version based on the Mk III hatchback Granada will doubtless become available in the near future.

Ford themselves, offer front spoilers, side-sills and rear boot spoiler for the Granada, with RS wheels completing the package. The end result is a much visually improved car.

One ''kit'' which Ford had produced, of which there aren't any copies (yet), is for the Transit, called Super Van II. This was built for Ford's European Truck operations by Auto Racing Technology of Woolaston. This vehicle contained a 3.9 litre Ford Cosworth DFL V8, capable of producing 590 bhp. It had a Hewland five-speed gearbox, independent suspension front and rear, and a top speed of over 180 mph. The 0-60 time was around 3 seconds and the price tag on the beast, if you wanted to buy one, was around £100,000. Perhaps the ultimate in ultra-personalised transport!

What does the future hold in store? The trends set by body kit manufacturers will

The Super Van II. This Transit has been described as the "fastest delivery van in the world". The carbon fibre reinforced body houses independent front and rear suspensions, five-speed Hewland gearbox and a mid-mounted 3.9-litre Cosworth V8. This produces around 590 bhp giving a 0-60 time of three seconds (0-100 in 6.5 seconds) and a top speed of over 180 mph! The van was built by Auto Racing Technology for Ford's European Truck Operation at a reputed cost of £100,000. With its racing body kit attached, it has lapped Silverstone at an average speed of 108.7 mph. This vehicle supersedes Super Van I, built in the 70s and powered by a 435 hp Gurney-Weslake engine giving 137 mph top speed (courtesy Ford Motor Company).

almost certainly continue in favour for some considerable time. The next few years will undoubtedly see a wider range of models catered for, with probable improvements in quality and materials of construction. We may see the introduction of such high-quality exotic materials such as polyimides, carbon-fibre and glass/Kevlar composites. The potential market for Ford-based body kits is clearly enormous. Further designs will undoubtedly appear from a variety of sources, the only limiting factor being the imagination of the talented designers currently at work in this field. It will be interesting to view their future efforts!